Lutheranism
ALL ABOUT JESUS

Written by
Paul T. McCain

General Editor
Scot A. Kinnaman

CONCORDIA PUBLISHING HOUSE • SAINT LOUIS

Lutheranism 101 Books

Lutheranism 101
Lutheranism 101: **THE COURSE**
Lutheranism 101: **FOR KIDS**
Lutheranism 101: **THE LORD'S SUPPER**
Lutheranism 101: **HOLY BAPTISM**
Lutheranism 101: **WORSHIP**

Copyright © 2017 Concordia Publishing House
3558 S. Jefferson Ave., St. Louis, MO 63118-3968
1-800-325-3040 • www.cph.org

Scripture quotations are from The Holy Bible, English Standard Version® (ESV®), copyright © 2001 by Crossway, a publishing ministry of Good News Publishers. Used by permission. All rights reserved.

Quotations from the Lutheran Confessions are from *Concordia: The Lutheran Confessions*, second edition; edited by Paul McCain, et al., copyright © 2006 Concordia Publishing House. All rights reserved.

Quotations from the Small Catechism are from *Luther's Small Catechism with Explanation*, copyright © 1986, 1991 Concordia Publishing House. All rights reserved.

Hymn texts with the abbreviation *LSB* are from *Lutheran Service Book*, copyright © 2006 Concordia Publishing House. All rights reserved.

The quotation from Augustine on p. 21 is from *Sancti Aurelii Augustini Hipponensis Episcopi, Opera Omni, Tomus Primus, Confessionum,* Liber I, in Jacques Paul Migne. *Patrologiae Cursus Completus. Series Latina).* Translated by Paul T. McCain, 2016.

Manufactured in the United States of America

1 2 3 4 5 6 7 8 9 10   26 25 24 23 22 21 20 19 18 17

Contents

Part Three: What Jesus Does for You, Then and Now

Conclusion: Why Is Lutheranism All About Jesus?

Putting It All Together: Christian Meditation: Focusing on Jesus

Appendices

Visit lutheranism101.com to download the free Leader Guide.

Foreword

Lutheranism 101 books give you usable and comprehensive overviews of what Lutherans believe and teach. These beliefs rest upon the foundational discussions of who God is, who man is, and who Jesus is. Along the way, and because faith does not happen in isolation, the series also presents how this faith is confessed in what Lutherans do, both in their corporate practice and in their personal piety.

After the release of the original *Lutheranism 101* book, numerous questions, comments, and suggestions were received, focusing on the meeting point between faith and practice. The *Lutheranism 101* series grew out of this correspondence. Each book in the series picks one topic and explores the basics of the Lutheran teaching in that area. The author also explores practice in that area, the understanding being that one necessarily informs the other.

The very title, *Lutheranism 101*, points forward to the learning and building up of the Christian faith through study and by participation in the Divine Service. *Lutheranism 101* encourages the use (and, dare we say, acquisition) of the basic resources for a Christian's study and growth: a Bible, Luther's Small Catechism, a hymnal, and, ultimately, the Lutheran Confessions.

A pastor was once asked, "Why do Lutherans talk about Jesus so much?" It was a revealing question, in a couple ways. First, much of modern American Christianity spends time talking about a lot of things other than Jesus. Second, it is a hallmark of Lutheranism that we talk so much about Jesus! *All About Jesus* expands on the topic from *Lutheranism 101*, presenting the classic teachings about the person and the work of Jesus Christ, going into detail about His incarnation, His life, His miracles, His suffering, His death and resurrection, and what all these things mean for all people. The more we know about Jesus, the more we understand the enormity of who He is and what He has done, the more we will want to talk about Jesus with others.

Each chapter concludes with several questions that can be used to further the study of and discussion about the material. For those who may be leading a group discussion based upon these chapters and for those individuals who want to check their answers against the author's comments, a free downloadable guide is available online at lutheranism101.com.

Introduction

Christianity: All About Jesus

Christianity has always been all about Jesus. Jesus Christ is the bedrock of the Christian faith. Jesus Christ is the entire reason the Christian Church exists to this very day and hour. When a church wavers from its commitment to the confession that Jesus Christ is the Son of God and the Savior of the world, it grows weak and sick, nearly unto death. The important question every person must answer is the question Jesus asked His first followers, "Who do you say that I am?" (Matthew 16:15). No matter if you know very little about Jesus or have spent a lifetime following Him, there is always more to know. But knowledge is not the goal. The goal is an ever-growing relationship with Jesus by His grace through faith. **You can never have enough Jesus, for Jesus always has more for you.**

The Reformation: All About Jesus

At the time of the Reformation, the biblical teachings about Jesus had become obscured with layers of human teachings. Instead of knowing Jesus as the Son of God who was sent by a loving and merciful God to save us from our sins, people were looking to Jesus with fear and dread, seeing Him as a great lawgiver and judge. Maybe, they thought, they could go to Jesus' mother, Mary, and plead with her to ask her son to be merciful. Perhaps, they hoped, if they gave money to support worship services offered on behalf of

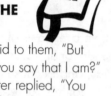

FROM THE BIBLE

He said to them, "But who do you say that I am?" Simon Peter replied, "You are the Christ, the Son of the living God." (Matthew 16:15–16)

BELIEVE, TEACH, CONFESS

To be baptized in God's name is to be baptized not by men, but by God Himself. Therefore, although it is performed by human hands, it is still truly God's own work. From this fact everyone may readily conclude that Baptism is a far higher work than any work performed by a man or a saint. For what work can we do that is greater than God's work? (LC IV 10) their dead relatives and others, God would have mercy on them when they died. God might even show kindness to their relatives already suffering purgatory. Purgatory is described as a kind of way station on the path to heaven; after death, a person would become "pure enough" to enter the perfection of heaven. The abuses in the Church at the time are well documented, and the Lutheran Reformation came about mostly as a result of a pastoral concern that people were not hearing the Gospel. The people needed to hear the Good News of God's love and mercy, given as free gifts to us, because of Jesus Christ. The people needed to understand that the Church is all about Jesus.

The Scriptures: All About Jesus

As you read this book, you'll notice that everything said about Jesus is backed up with references to the Holy Scriptures. Christianity is based on the eye- and ear-witness testimonies of those who lived and worked with Jesus during His earthly life. Most of the writers of the New Testament personally witnessed His execution by crucifixion and saw Him alive and well after He had been buried. The accounts in the New Testament are also written by those who knew the eyewitnesses personally or who, like the apostle Paul, were given direct revelations from the risen Christ. The accounts about Jesus match to an astonishing degree. Packed into the pages of the New Testament are truths that help us examine the person and the work of Jesus of Nazareth and come to firm conclusions about what He did, who He is, and what His life and work mean for us to this day.

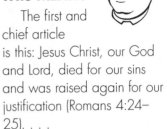

WHAT DOES THIS MEAN?

The first and chief article is this: Jesus Christ, our God and Lord, died for our sins and was raised again for our justification (Romans 4:24–25). . . .

Upon this article everything that we teach and practice depends, in opposition to the pope, the devil, and the whole world. Therefore, we must be certain and not doubt this doctrine. Otherwise, all is lost, and the pope, the devil, and all adversaries win the victory and the right over us. (SA III 1, 5)

FROM THE BIBLE

These [things] are written so that you may believe that Jesus is the Christ, the Son of God, and that by believing you may have life in His name. (John 20:31)

Abbreviations

AE	Luther, Martin. *Luther's Works*. American Edition. Volumes 1–30: Edited by Jaroslav Pelikan. St. Louis: Concordia, 1955–76. Volumes 31–55: Edited by Helmut Lehmann. Philadelphia/Minneapolis: Muhlenberg/Fortress, 1957–86. Volumes 56–75: Edited by Christopher Boyd Brown and Benjamin T. G. Mayes. St. Louis: Concordia, 2009–.
LSB	*Lutheran Service Book*. St. Louis: Concordia, 2006.
Lutheranism 101	Kinnaman, Scot A., gen. ed. *Lutheranism 101*. St. Louis: Concordia, 2010.
TLSB	*The Lutheran Study Bible*. St. Louis: Concordia, 2009.

Lutheran Confessions

You will see many quotations from the Lutheran Confessions as found in the Book of Concord. The following list provides abbreviations used, what they mean, and examples of how you would find the text. Except for Small Catechism quotations, the English translations of the Lutheran Confessions cited in this book come from *Concordia: The Lutheran Confessions*, 2nd ed. (St. Louis: Concordia, 2006).

- AC Augsburg Confession
- Ap Apology of the Augsburg Confession
- BEC Appendix B: A Brief Exhortation to Confession
- Ep Epitome of the Formula of Concord
- FC Formula of Concord
- SA Smalcald Articles
- SC Small Catechism
- SD Solid Declaration of the Formula of Concord
- Tr Treatise on the Power and Primacy of the Pope

Examples:

AC XX 4	(Augsburg Confession, Article XX, paragraph 4)
Ap IV 229	(Apology of the AC, Article IV, paragraph 229)

FC SD X 24   (Solid Declaration of the Formula of Concord, Article X, paragraph 24)

FC Ep V 8   (Epitome of the Formula of Concord, Article V, paragraph 8)

LC V 32, 37   (Large Catechism, Part 5, paragraphs 32 and 37)

SA III I 6   (Smalcald Articles, Part III, Article I, paragraph 6)

SC III 5   (Small Catechism, Part III, paragraph 5)

Tr 5   (Treatise, paragraph 5)

NAVIGATING LUTHERANISM 101

WHAT DOES THIS MEAN?

Quotes from Martin Luther

MAKING CONNECTIONS

Connecting theology, faith, and life

NEED TO KNOW

Terms and phrases quickly defined

FROM THE BIBLE

Quotations from, well, the Bible

TECHNICAL STUFF

Big theological concepts in bite-size pieces

BELIEVE, TEACH, CONFESS

Quotations from the Lutheran Confessions

In the Creeds, We Confess Jesus

A creed (from the Latin *credo*, "I believe") is a confession of faith used by individual Christians, congregations, and churches to give voice to what is believed, taught, and confessed about God. For detailed information on the history and usage of the following creeds, see Chapter 31, "We Confess," in *Lutheranism 101.*

Apostles' Creed

The Apostles' Creed is the oldest of the three most historic and traditional Christian creeds. The Apostles' Creed is often called the Baptismal Creed. It is commonly used in worship services where Holy Communion is not being celebrated, in small groups, and for individual prayer.

I believe in God, the Father Almighty,
  maker of heaven and earth.
And in Jesus Christ, His only Son, our Lord,
   who was conceived by the Holy Spirit,
   born of the virgin Mary,
   suffered under Pontius Pilate,
   was crucified, died and was buried.
   He descended into hell.
   The third day He rose again from the dead.
   He ascended into heaven
   and sits at the right hand of God, the Father Almighty.
   From thence He will come to judge the living and the dead.
I believe in the Holy Spirit,
   the holy Christian Church,
      the communion of saints,
   the forgiveness of sins,
   the resurrection of the body,
   and the life everlasting. Amen.

Nicene Creed

The Nicene Creed was developed to respond to controversies over the doctrine of the Trinity and the deity of Jesus Christ. As a result, the Nicene Creed talks more about Jesus and His relationship with the Father and the Holy Spirit. The Nicene Creed is used in worship services when Holy Communion is celebrated.

I believe in one God,
   the Father Almighty,
   maker of heaven and earth
      and of all things visible and invisible.

And in one Lord Jesus Christ,
   the only-begotten Son of God,
   begotten of His Father before all worlds,
   God of God, Light of Light,
   very God of very God,
   begotten, not made,
   being of one substance with the Father,
   by whom all things were made;
   who for us men and for our salvation came down from heaven
   and was incarnate by the Holy Spirit of the virgin Mary and was made man;
   and was crucified also for us under Pontius Pilate.
   He suffered and was buried.
   And the third day He rose again according to the Scriptures
      and ascended into heaven
   and sits at the right hand of the Father.
   And He will come again with glory to judge both the living and the dead,
   whose kingdom will have no end.

And I believe in the Holy Spirit,
   the Lord and giver of life,
   who proceeds from the Father and the Son,
   who with the Father and Son together is worshiped and glorified,
   who spoke by the prophets.
   And I believe in one holy Christian and apostolic Church,
   I acknowledge one Baptism for the remission of sins,
   and I look for the resurrection of the dead
   and the life of the world to come. Amen.

Athanasian Creed

Although never officially adopted by the Church, the Athanasian Creed affirms Christian beliefs, especially Christ's divinity and His equality with the persons of the Holy Trinity.

Whoever desires to be saved must, above all, hold the catholic faith.

Whoever does not keep it whole and undefiled will without doubt perish eternally.

And the catholic faith is this,

that we worship one God in Trinity and Trinity in Unity, neither confusing the persons nor dividing the substance.

For the Father is one person, the Son is another, and the Holy Spirit is another.

But the Godhead of the Father and of the Son and of the Holy Spirit is one: the glory equal, the majesty coeternal.

Such as the Father is, such is the Son, and such is the Holy Spirit:

the Father uncreated, the Son uncreated, the Holy Spirit uncreated;

the Father infinite, the Son infinite, the Holy Spirit infinite;

the Father eternal, the Son eternal, the Holy Spirit eternal.

And yet there are not three Eternals, but one Eternal,

just as there are not three Uncreated or three Infinites, but one Uncreated and one Infinite.

In the same way, the Father is almighty, the Son almighty, the Holy Spirit almighty;

and yet there are not three Almighties, but one Almighty.

So the Father is God, the Son is God, the Holy Spirit is God;

and yet there are not three Gods, but one God.

So the Father is Lord, the Son is Lord, the Holy Spirit is Lord;

and yet there are not three Lords, but one Lord.

Just as we are compelled by the Christian truth to acknowledge each distinct person as God and Lord, so also are we prohibited by the catholic religion to say that there are three Gods or Lords.

The Father is not made nor created nor begotten by anyone.

The Son is neither made nor created, but begotten of the Father alone.

The Holy Spirit is of the Father and of the Son, neither made nor created nor begotten, but proceeding.

Thus, there is one Father, not three Fathers; one Son, not three Sons; one Holy Spirit, not three Holy Spirits.

And in this Trinity none is before or after another; none is greater or less than another;

but the whole three persons are coeternal with each other and coequal, so that in all things, as has been stated above, the Trinity in Unity and Unity in Trinity is to be worshiped.

Therefore, whoever desires to be saved must think thus about the Trinity.

But it is also necessary for everlasting salvation that one faithfully believe the incarnation of our Lord Jesus Christ.

Therefore, it is the right faith that we believe and confess that our Lord Jesus Christ, the Son of God, is at the same time both God and man.

He is God, begotten from the substance of the Father before all ages; and He is man, born from the substance of His mother in this age:

perfect God and perfect man, composed of a rational soul and human flesh;

equal to the Father with respect to His divinity, less than the Father with respect to His humanity.

Although He is God and man, He is not two, but one Christ:

one, however, not by the conversion of the divinity into flesh, but by the assumption of the humanity into God;

one altogether, not by confusion of substance, but by unity of person.

For as the rational soul and flesh is one man, so God and man is one Christ,

who suffered for our salvation, descended into hell, rose again the third day from the dead,

ascended into heaven, and is seated at the right hand of the Father, God Almighty, from whence He will come to judge the living and the dead.

At His coming all people will rise again with their bodies and give an account concerning their own deeds.

And those who have done good will enter into eternal life, and those who have done evil into eternal fire.

This is the catholic faith; whoever does not believe it faithfully and firmly cannot be saved.

PART ONE

What you'll learn about:

- "Shocking" truths taught in Christianity.
- The real meaning of Christianity.
- What the various names of Jesus are and what they mean.
- That Jesus is a prophet, priest, and a king.

Why Is Christianity All About Jesus?

"Well, what else would it be about?" you might be asking. Most people not familiar with Christianity think it is really about Christians running around telling other people what they can or cannot do. And it is sad, but true, that many people have encountered only harsh judgment and condemnation and little love and compassion from the Church. But is that what Christianity is all about? Loving your neighbors? Sadly, too many Christians don't even have this clear in their minds. Let's take a closer look at why it is all about Jesus.

CHAPTER 1

There's a Reason It's Called "CHRISTianity"

In This Chapter

- Christianity is all about Jesus.
- Salvation can be found nowhere else.
- The real meaning of Christianity.

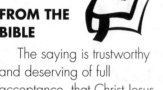

FROM THE BIBLE

In Antioch the disciples were first called Christians. (Acts 11:26)

Where They Were First Called Christians

It may seem obvious, but we need to make clear what often becomes lost in the shuffle. Christianity really is all about Jesus. Numerous Christian denominations and movements have walked away from their confidence in the trustworthiness of the Bible. As a result, they are no longer comfortable with traditional teachings about Jesus. But the fact remains that Christianity is all about Christ Jesus—the one who came into this world to save sinners and give them new life. New life is not simply a future time in the "great beyond" but something we receive and experience right here, right now, while we are yet living on earth. The fact that we are made children of God by grace through faith in Christ shapes the way we live our lives. It forms and shapes our attitudes toward ourselves and toward others. No matter what comes, we are God's loved children.

FROM THE BIBLE

The saying is trustworthy and deserving of full acceptance, that Christ Jesus came into the world to save sinners, of whom I am the foremost. (1 Timothy 1:15)

Jesus Himself makes the bold claim, "I am the way, and the truth, and the life. No one comes to the Father except through Me" (John 14:6). Look carefully at that claim. It's crazy, right? That's what many people in Jesus' day, and still today, say when they hear such an exclusive claim. They think, "Really, Jesus? Are You nuts? You're really telling me that You, and You alone, are the way, the truth, and the life? You really expect me to believe that the only way to get to heaven is through You? What kind of arrogant fool would make such a claim? What kind of crazy person would believe such a thing?

An Exclusive Name with Exclusive Claims

In Jesus' day, His exclusive claims got Him into trouble—so much trouble, in fact, that the people who first heard Christ ended up killing Him. Why? Because He claimed to be the Son of God, the promised Messiah. The Hebrew word for *Messiah* is *Mashiach*. It means "the anointed one" and it was translated into the Greek language as *Christos* (*Xristos*) hence the word in English, *Christ*. Jesus was appointed by God to be the world's Savior. But despite the threats of death, Jesus never backed away from His mission and from His message. He prayed to His Father in heaven, "This is eternal life, that they know You, the only true God, and Jesus Christ whom You have sent" (John 17:3).

Christianity is all about Jesus because He, and He alone, is the only source of salvation and life and hope and lasting joy. The apostle Peter said, "There is salvation in no one else, for there is no other name under heaven given among men by which we must be saved" (Acts 4:12). Peter's assertion was regarded as offensive, even crazy, and it still is today. We often hear people say, "Don't we all pray to the same God? Aren't all religions on the same path to heaven? Doesn't God reveal Himself in many different ways and all that matters is whether you are a good person?" Answer: No. Absolutely not.

MAKING CONNECTIONS

Let the humble pilgrim look at Christ. . . . Behold he who wants to go, has the way, for Christ is the way, and whither he wants to go, for Christ is the truth, and where he wants to abide, for Christ is the life. —John Hus (*The Church*, p. 90; quoted in *TLSB* on John 14:6, p. 1811)

WHAT DOES THIS MEAN?

Close your eyes, and say: "I know nothing of God or of the Father unless I come here and listen to Christ." For anything preached or invented outside this Man's Word, no matter what it may be or how sublime it may sound, is not the Father, but remains blindness, error, yes, the devil himself. (AE 23:351)

The Real Meaning and Purpose of Christianity

The most important message and purpose of Christianity is not to impart helpful tips for better living or for self-improvement. Christianity is not a club for "good people." No, in fact, Christianity is all about bringing sick, broken, weak, weary, hurting, troubled, sinful people to the only One who can make them whole, restore them to health, forgive all their sins, and set them on the path to eternal life with Him in heaven.

> **TECHNICAL STUFF**
>
> The Greek word for *Church* is *ekklesia*, which means "assembly," literally, "ones who are called out." The Greek word for *fellowship* is *koinonia*, which means to have things in common. Those who have fellowship are sharing things together.

Some Christians today, for various reasons, regard Church as a training or fitness center, a place where they go to get a great spiritual workout and to bulk up their "spiritual lives." While we do indeed receive strength and hope through the message of Jesus and His Good News, the Church is actually more like a hospital into which people are brought by our Savior, Jesus Christ, and taken care of, nurtured and healed, cleansed and pardoned. In this community, we are all "recovering sinners" until the very moment of death. We are called "Christians" because all that we are and all that we will be someday after death is because of Christ and Him crucified.

And so we have before us the facts from Scripture. Not only can we understand those facts; we must understand those facts. But knowledge of the facts about Jesus and knowledge about the Christian faith is not the goal. Knowledge only goes so far. Knowing facts is one thing, but trusting in the truths they reveal is quite another. In fact, it is a gift from God that we call "faith." We need to cling to these facts for what they really are—life-saving and life-giving truths that give our entire life meaning and purpose and that serve us every day in every way.

Jesus Is the Way

How many "ways" are you tempted to follow to find happiness, peace, joy, and tranquility? Many follow the way of drugs, alcohol, sex, money, or anything else you want to add to that list. But Jesus is "the way" back home to our heavenly Father. He is the way out of our slavery to sin. Scripture is very clear that when we embrace the way of Christ, we are embracing the way of life and escaping from the way that leads only to torment and destruction in eternal separation from God. To follow Jesus is to find ourselves on the way that leads to eternal life. But make no mistake, Christianity is not simply an insurance policy we can buy and tuck away in a safe-deposit box for use someday. Christianity is not like those fire alarms we see in buildings that say, "IN THE CASE OF EMERGENCY BREAK GLASS." No, Christianity was called "the Way" because it is a way of life, right here and right now.

St. Paul explains in Romans 6:

> What shall we say then? Are we to continue in sin that grace may abound? By no means! How can we who died to sin still live in it? Do you not know that all of us who have been baptized into Christ Jesus were baptized into His death? We were buried therefore with Him by baptism into death, in order that, just as Christ was raised from the dead by the glory of the Father, we too might walk in newness of life. (vv. 1–4)

Consider Paul's words carefully. Christ sets us on the way that leads to eternal life because He alone is that way. And that way not only rescues us from the eternal punishment we all deserve for sin, but it also rescues us from the power of sin in our lives right now. We are not simply doomed to failure. In Christ, we have been raised to a new life. What is this "new life"? It is one in which we are not gripped by hopelessness and helplessness to change or find peace from a guilty conscience or the burden of a vexing and reoccurring activity that is contrary to God's Word. We are given a new life that does not chain us to our past. It does not make us look to physical possessions for happiness or leave us as merely pawns on some large cosmic chest board. A new life in Christ finds its meaning and purpose in being loved deeply by Christ and, in turn, shows and reflects that love to all those around us. A new life is a life anchored in the love, mercy, and peace of God through Jesus Christ. You can now boldly say, "Satan, get out of my way, for it is the way of Christ Jesus my Lord. No, I will not follow the way you would have me go. I know where that leads. I am following the way of my Lord Jesus Christ."

Jesus Is the Truth

Again, what a blessing it is to study the truths revealed in God's Word. We dig deeply into the teachings (the doctrines) revealed in Scripture to get at the truth that is Jesus Christ. As Paul exclaims in Romans 3:4: "Let God be true though every one were a liar." Anything that conflicts with the truths of God's Word is a lie. The truth of Christ is objectively true. It is truth aside from how you or I feel about it. The truths of Christ do not rest on the shaky foundation of human feeling, emotion, or opinion. Some days you may feel close to Christ; His truths may wash over you with overwhelming power as you hear the Gospel preached in a particularly meaningful way at just the right time. You may sing a hymn and be struck deeply by the truth of God's Word expressed in it. Other days you may feel far from God. You may experience in a heavy way the memory of past sins. Doubt and guilt may plague you at times. But do these negative feelings make the good of Jesus for you any less true? Are you really "less" of a Christian based on how you feel? Absolutely not.

And because this truth is objectively yours, every aspect of that truth is something you can personally hold on to for dear life. Literally! Consider how Paul explains how Christ, the truth, fully impacts and changes your life to the point that as a child of God, by the grace of God, you now are able to "present your bodies as a living sacrifice, holy and acceptable to God, which is your spiritual worship. Do not be conformed to this world, but be transformed by the renewal of your mind, that by testing you may discern what is the will of God, what is good and acceptable and perfect" (Romans 12:1–3). The truth that is Christ becomes your truth, and the Holy Spirit enables you now to live in that truth and to reject being conformed to the world's standards of what is "truth" or what makes life meaningful. You are able now, in the light of Christ's truth, to evaluate and discern what actually is true and what is not, and therefore understand what is acceptable to God and what is not.

Christ, who is the truth, shows you the truth of who you were without Him and who you are now that you have been made new in Him. You are set free to love, to serve, and to live out your life as His new creation. You have the truth that sets you free from your former self, guides and shapes your every day here in this life, and leads you on your pilgrimage to your heavenly home. Troubles will come. Pain will be part of your life. Yes, you will stumble and fall into sin, but you know the truth of Jesus Christ: He who is faithful and just will forgive you and cleanse you from all unrighteousness (1 John 1:9), set you back on your feet, and turn you back to His truth.

Jesus Is the Life

"If anyone is in Christ, he is a new creation. The old has passed away; behold, the new has come" (2 Corinthians 5:17). Savor these words from God. They are not talking only about something in the future or the past. They describe your life now in Christ. How is Christ the life? He is the one who gave up His life so you might now have a new life. He laid down His life so you could put on the new life He gives to you as a pure and gracious gift. The "old life" that you were condemned to live in the body now—a life of absolute slavery to sin and its power over you—is done away with.

What is the "good life"? Throughout the ages, philosophers have debated, analyzed, and examined that question from every angle, exhausting the limits of human reason to provide a satisfying answer. But there is no answer that satisfies anyone completely unless he or she comes to the realization that Christ is the life! Our culture bombards us constantly with the promise that if only we get this, or do this, or know this person, or go here, or watch this, or drink this, or take this drug, or . . . if only we . . . , then we will know the good life. Then we will be happy. Then we will find fulfillment.

In what would become the first written spiritual autobiography, Augustine, a fourth-century theologian and church leader, wrote a brutally honest self-assessment. He titled the book *The Confessions*, and in it he holds nothing back. His purpose was to explain how he found true life, real life and abundant life, only in Jesus Christ, who is Himself "the life." Can you identify with Augustine?

MAKING CONNECTIONS

Each day you arise to a new life. Each day commend yourself to the gracious care of God. Luther's morning prayer, found in the Small Catechism, is a good way to begin. Make the sign of the cross and say:

"I thank You, my heavenly Father, through Jesus Christ, Your dear Son, that You have kept me this night from all harm and danger; and I pray that You would keep me this day also from sin and every evil, that all my doings and life may please You. For into Your hands I commend myself, my body and soul, and all things. Let Your holy angel be with me, that the evil foe may have no power over me. Amen."

> O Lord, You are great and greatly worthy of being praised. Your power is enormous, and Your wisdom beyond comprehension. We humans, being part of Your creation, want to praise You. We carry around our mortality. We see our sin and the proof that You resist the proud. Yet, we still deeply desire to praise You. You move us to delight in praising You. You have made us for Yourself. Our hearts are restless until they rest in You.

The good life is found only when we rest in God. And we rest in God because Jesus Christ, our Good Shepherd, has brought us into the good and green pastures of salvation. In this life, in this new life, in Christ who is *the* life, we find our rest, here in time, and forever in eternity.

Two of the Most Ancient Symbols Used by Christians

To understand how consistently passionate the Church has been about bearing clear and truthful witness to Christ, we need to go back to the earliest years of the Church's history. We must return to the time when the Church was considered a dangerous movement to the established order. We must go back to when Christians were often forced to meet in relative secrecy and only admitted people to membership in a congregation after two or three years of rigorous instruction and training.

The year is AD 150. Throughout the Roman Empire there is relative peace, from the far northern reaches of the British Isles, to northwestern frontiers in the lands of the German barbarians, across what we today call Europe, throughout Asia Minor and the Mideast, and all along North Africa. It is the closing era of the great *Pax Romana*, the "Roman Peace," which has been imposed by sheer military might, but with a particularly brilliant way of pacifying conquered peoples for many hundreds of years: allow them to retain many of their local customs and beliefs, just as long as they acknowledged the supremacy of the Roman Caesar as both lord and god. Roman Emperors even came to be referred to as "the Son of God." Christians suffered intense persecution under the rule of several Caesars, who demanded Christians take an oath of faithfulness to the Roman Emperor and offer up a pinch of incense as a form of emperor worship. Thousands of early Christians suffered death rather than compromise their confession that only Christ is to be worshiped as the Son of God.

This placed members of religious faiths who opposed any such false confession of faith at great risk, first the Jews in Palestine, who were conquered and pacified decisively around AD 70, and then the fledgling movement that we know today as Christianity. But by 150, Christians were found in every major city and territory of the Roman Empire, even in the city of Rome itself. And they had developed a secret "code" by which they would be able to identify one another quietly without risk of being found out by the authorities. They chose a simple drawing of a fish as one of their symbols, along with an eight-spoked wheel.

The ICHTHUS Fish

The ancient Christian symbol of a fish was scrawled on walls and would often be silently traced in the dirt as people met, to identify them as followers of Jesus Christ, God's Son, the Savior. Here is how it worked.

The symbol was simple:

Why a fish? There was a hidden message in this symbol for those who followed Christ. The Greek word for "fish" is *Ichthus*, or in Greek letters ΙΧΘΥΣ. Those letters in the Greek word for fish created an acrostic, a word puzzle of sorts where letters in each line form a word or words. ΙΧΘΥΣ (*Ichthus*) is an acrostic where the first letters stand for "Ἰησοῦς Χριστός, Θεοῦ Υἱός, Σωτήρ" or, "Jesus Christ, God's Son, Savior."

Here's how it works:

> ΙΧΘΥΣ (*Ichthus*) is an acrostic for
> "Ἰησοῦς Χριστός, Θεοῦ Υἱός, Σωτήρ"
> Ἰησοῦς, **I**ēsous = Jesus
> Χριστός, **Ch**ristos = Christ
> Θεοῦ, **Th**eou = God's
> Υἱός, **Hu**ios = Son
> Σωτήρ, **S**ōtēr = Savior

Here's how it might be pictured:

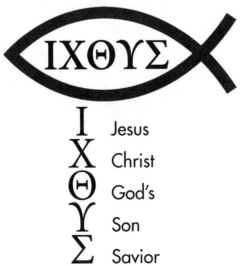

I Jesus
X Christ
Θ God's
Υ Son
Σ Savior

The ICHTHUS Eight-Spoked Wheel

An eight-spoked wheel was also used as a symbol for this ancient Christian confession, again, based on the ΙΧΘΥΣ (*Ichthus*), the Greek letters for fish. How this works:

ΙΧΘΥΣ

We find these symbols scattered around the ruins of the ancient Roman world, with notable examples in the city of Ephesus. The symbol and its meaning reveal that from the very beginning of the Christian faith it has been all about Jesus. You may think, "Of course Christianity is all about Jesus!" But as we will learn, throughout the history of the Church, it has been a constant temptation to take our eyes off of Jesus. We let our eyes wander and become distracted to the point that finally Jesus is removed from the center of Christianity and replaced with something else.

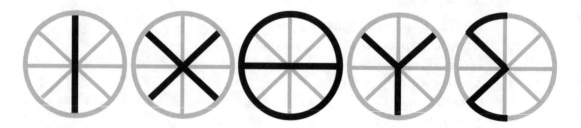

Study Questions

1. What is the most important message and purpose of Christianity?

2. What is the Hebrew word for *Messiah*, and what does it mean? Why is it an appropriate name for Jesus?

3. What is the purpose of church?

4. There is a big difference between knowing facts from Scripture and trusting in the truths they reveal. Is one more important than the other? Explain.

5. How do you know what is acceptable to God and what is not?

6. In the Early Church, people were admitted to the church only after two or three years of rigorous instruction and training. Why? To what extent is this practice continued today?

Discussion Questions

1. Why have so many Christian denominations walked away from their confidence in the trustworthiness of the Bible? What are the dangers in doing so?

2. How does the fact that you are made a child of God by grace through faith in Christ shape the way you live your life? What evidence is there that you are a child of God?

3. How can you respond to the claim that "God reveals Himself in many different ways, and all that really matters is whether you're a good person"?

4. The truths of Christ do not rest on the foundation of human feeling, emotion, or opinion. If that is the case, then why is it so easy for Christians to fall prey to their feelings, emotions, and opinions when it comes to their faith?

Visit lutheranism101.com to download the free Leader Guide.

CHAPTER 2

There Are Only Two Religions in the World

MAKING CONNECTIONS

So about that bumper sticker . . . yes, we must coexist with everyone around us. Christians are not called to wage some kind of holy war against opposing points of view. We do not convert people at the point of a sword or the end of a gun. The Christian is **in** the world, but not **of** the world. But the intellectual dishonesty in the bumper sticker is simply the lie that in fact all religions are equal and that all equally teach the same things. In fact, they do not, and it is dishonest to pretend that they do.

In This Chapter

- False: all religions are separate but equal.
- True: there are only two religions.
- There is no Christianity without Jesus.

Coexist? Yes. Coequal? No.

We see them everywhere, the "Coexist" bumper stickers that use symbols of various world religions to spell out the word *coexist*. It would be nice to think that everyone displaying those bumper stickers is simply advocating that all people act respectfully toward one another and not violently persecute people just because of what they believe. Yes, it would be nice to think so. But the "coexist" bumper sticker is mostly a reflection of the common opinion that "all religions are the same," that "we are all on the same road to heaven," and that "we each worship God as we understand Him," with all views about God being equally valid and true. The insidious flip side of the thought is, ironically, the attitude that the only thing to not be tolerated is an exclusive claim to truth.

But Christianity is an exclusive truth-claim that absolutely rules out the possibility that there ever was, is, or ever will be a way to God that does not begin, continue, and end through the person and work of Jesus Christ. This is an incredibly unpopular opinion today. Voice this view and you may well be laughed at, ridiculed, or shouted down. In many places in the world, admitting to being a Christian brings severe repercussions, even death. And thus it has always been. Simply put: Know Jesus, know God. No Jesus, no God.

FROM THE BIBLE

Jesus said to him, "I am the way, and the truth, and the life. No one comes to the Father except through Me. If you had known Me, you would have known My Father also. From now on you do know Him and have seen Him." (John 14:6–7)

John 14:6–7 is essential for our understanding and discussion. Specifically, look at verse 7: "If you had known Me, you would have known My Father also." Yes, this is the common fate of all human beings. Without knowing Jesus Christ, none of us can ever know the Father. We obtain hints of His power and greatness as we survey the majesty of His creation, but, frankly, it would not be too long until we came to the following conclusions: (1) He must be very angry at us to allow all of these natural disasters; (2) as we peer ever more deeply into space via various technologies, it seems that God must be vastly removed from us; and (3) as we look in more detail at the very substance of life, gazing via technology at the atom itself, looking for "the God particle" as it has come to be known, it seems that God is utterly unknowable and complex.

Without Jesus Christ, that would be the extent of what we would know about God—and what a sad knowledge that would be. But in Jesus Christ, as Jesus Himself says, "From now on you do know Him and have seen Him" (John 14:7). This is the very reason God sent His Son into the world, to reveal Himself to the world. When we see Jesus, we gaze upon God as He wishes to be seen. As we come to know Jesus, we come to know God as He wants us to know Him.

And what kind of God is it that we find and see and know? A God of infinite compassion and love. For this reason, the apostle John and all of Scripture summarizes and captures the very being of God with one word: love. "God is love" (1 John 4:8). The chief quality, attribute, and characteristic of God is not "glory" or "sovereignty" or "judgment" or "anger" or "power." No, above everything else, God is love. "For God so loved the world, that He gave His only Son, that whoever believes in Him should not perish but have eternal life" (John 3:16). Cling then to Jesus Christ, and you have the Father. You are deeply loved.

There Are Only Two Religions

Only two? Yes, you read that right. There is the religion of man's making and there is the religion of God's own self-revelation through Jesus, His Son. The world's most popular religion, no matter what particular name it may have, is the religion of works and the Law. It is the religion in which human beings search for God, reach out to Him, try to maintain a relationship with Him, and seek to win His favor by their good works. This is extremely popular and always has been. We see this clearly in all of the world's religions that, in various ways, are about what human beings can do for God to make Him love and accept them or grant their wishes.

True Christianity is utterly devoid of any such sentiment. It is all about God reaching out to humankind in love and making the first move to restore what was lost, to rescue that which was dying, to renew what had been corrupted by sin, death, and the devil. Even the word *religion* does not do justice to what Christianity is. Remember that it was first described as "the Way." The way of what? The way of life! The key to understanding Christianity is to understand that it is all about Jesus. Jesus tells us that He is the way, the truth, and the life. He is the way because He is the truth. As a result, He gives us life abundantly!

Far too many people have been led to believe that Christianity is mostly about a system of morals and ethics, behaviors, lifestyles, personal choices, self-help and self-improvement, getting to know the real you, a way to earn your way to heaven, or something of the like. Now surely, the Christian "way" does involve a unique approach to morals and ethics and behaviors and lifestyles and choices, but that all comes after the main thing about Christianity: God reaching out to claim you as His own dear child because of Jesus.

The more you get to know Jesus, the more you come to understand that He is indeed the one who comes looking for you because of who and what He is and what He has done.

FROM THE BIBLE

Then they said to Him, "What must we do, to be doing the works of God?" Jesus answered them, "This is the work of God, that you believe in Him whom He has sent." (John 6:28–29)

They exchanged the truth about God for a lie and worshiped and served the creature rather than the Creator, who is blessed forever! Amen. (Romans 1:25)

But if it is by grace, it is no longer on the basis of works; otherwise grace would no longer be grace. (Romans 11:6)

A Brief Overview of Three of the World Largest Religions

Islam

After Christianity, Islam is the world's second largest religion, with over 1.7 billion adherents. The Qur'an is regarded by Muslims to be the actual holy words of Allah (the Arabic word for "God"). The Arabic language of the Qur'an is regarded to be as holy and divine by Muslims as are the body and blood of Christ under the bread and wine of the Lord's Supper by Christians. For Muslims, the holy text of the Qur'an was given directly by God to the prophet Muhammad, whom Muslims regard to be the last and greatest prophet of God. They also regard Abraham, Moses, and Jesus to be God's prophets. Islam arose in the early part of the seventh century AD and spread rapidly across most of the nations of what we know today as the Middle East and has spread throughout Africa and Asia as well, with Muslim communities now found throughout the world and in ever increasing numbers in the Americas and Europe. The two major "denominations" of Islam include Sunni Islam (70–90%) and Shia (10–20%). The word *Islam* itself means "submission." The word *Muslim* derives from the word *Islam* and is used to refer to adherents of Islam. *Muslim* means "one who surrenders to the will of Allah."

The religion of Islam is deeply rooted in submission to the revelation of Allah in the Qur'an and regards obedient submission as the key to earning the favor and blessing of Allah. The idea that Allah is a personal loving heavenly father is alien to most of Islam. Islam emphasizes the monotheistic nature of Allah and the exclusive place of Muhammad as his prophet. Submission to Allah's will is ever most in the forefront of the Muslim worldview, achieved by rigorous obedience to the Qur'an and the various traditions and teachings of those regarded as authoritative interpreters and teachers of the traditions of Muhammad. Most Muslims regard these authoritative traditions to be the exclusive way to interpret and live out the Islamic religions.

A person's place in the afterlife depends entirely on obedience and good works during life on earth.

Hinduism

Hinduism is a religion found primarily throughout India and Nepal, though in the modern era it has spread worldwide as people have immigrated into other countries. It is the world's third largest religion, with over one billion adherents. It is often said to be the world's oldest religion. Hinduism is characterized by worship of a large variety of gods and goddesses and stresses living according to "the eternal law." It took on much of its present form around 500 BC.

Hinduism has texts regarded as sacred, both texts that are "heard" and those that are "remembered." The Hindu "scripture" includes the Vedas and Upanishads, the Bhagavad Gita and the Agamas. These texts do not play the same role in Hinduism as does the Bible for Christianity of the Qur'an for Islam, but are regarded as starting points to explore the nature of the divine, the origin of the world, and so on.

Hinduism emphasizes human behavior as a way to assure further progression and moral ascent toward the divine, by focusing on ethics (dharma), works (artha), controlling desires and passions (kama), liberation and freedom (moksha), and actions and consequences (karma). Hindus practice elaborate rituals of offering sacrifices to various gods, ritual washings, and recitation of sacred texts and phrases, known as mantras. Many Hindu festivals are observed. All Hindu actions are intended to earn favor with the divine. It is hard to pin down precisely what Hinduism believes about "God" since there are various opinions, ranging from many gods to no one god at all.

Each person is regarded as having an "atman" or spirit, which is said to be eternal. Various sects worship various gods, regarded as "Supreme Spirits," including Vishnu, Brahma, Shiva, or Shakti. Humans will be judged on the basis of their works. In Hinduism, there is nearly an overwhelming variety of gods, goddesses, and spiritual practices. As it is practiced by most adherents, human efforts are done to appease and please various gods and goddesses for favor in this life and for a spiritual existence to come after this life.

Buddhism

Buddhism originated in India and is traced back to the teachings of Siddhartha Gautama, known as "the Buddha" or "the enlightened one." Buddhists believe he lived and taught in India sometime between the sixth and fourth centuries BC. Buddhism spread throughout Asia and is the world's fourth largest religion, with some five hundred million followers.

Buddhists regard the Buddha as their ultimate teacher and the one whose example they strive to emulate. It is said that through meditation over a long period of time, involving a wide range of bodily self-discipline and control, the Buddha achieved the state of pure enlightenment while sitting under what is known as the "Bodhi Tree" in the town of Bodh Gaya, in Southern Asia. As a result of this long process of asceticism and meditation, the Buddha became an "enlightened being" and as a result attracted followers who spread his teachings.

It is impossible in this short summary to explain the wide variety of traditions and teachings of various branches and forms of Buddhism, but essential to Buddhism is the belief that enlightenment depends on one's behavior in one's current life-form and the belief that actions in this life have karmic consequences in the next. Mediation is a key practice of Buddhism, said to detach one from all sensory and earthly desires. Perhaps the most widely recognized symbol of Buddhism is the statues of the meditating Buddha. These statues can be very small or can be huge statues carved into the face of cliffs and mountains.

Again, the focus in this religion is on human activity and what we would term "good works" in order to achieve spiritual enlightenment. The concept of a loving God forgiving sins is a thought alien to Buddhism.

Study Questions

1. What are the dangers of the "coexist" movement? On the other hand, how are Christians to coexist with everyone around them?

2. Without knowing Jesus, what three conclusions do people ultimately believe about God?

3. As we come to know Jesus, what do we come to know about God?

4. What is the religion of man's making? Why is it so popular?

5. What is the main difference between Christianity and the religion of works and the Law?

Discussion Questions

1. Why do so many people, including Christians, believe that Christianity is mostly about trying to do more good than bad—that it's a system of morals and ethics, behaviors and lifestyles, and personal choices? Where does that belief come from?

2. What do you think attracts people to religions other than Christianity such as Islam, Hinduism, and Buddhism?

3. What does it mean to be "in" the world but not "of" the world?

4. Why are Christians who claim that Jesus is the only way to heaven often ridiculed and mocked, even persecuted and killed? How prepared are you to defend your Christian faith in the face of persecution?

Visit lutheranism101.com to download the free Leader Guide.

CHAPTER 3

What's in a Name?

In This Chapter

- *Jesus* is a name above every name.
- Jesus is "set apart" as the Savior.
- Names and titles confess who Jesus is.

NEED TO KNOW

Jesus: The personal name of the Second Person of the Trinity after His conception and birth. It means "Yahweh saves."

TECHNICAL STUFF

Trinity is the word we use to describe the fact that there is one God, and yet that one God is three persons. *Triune* comes from the Latin word that means "Three in one." There are not three gods, nor is there only one person who appears to us in three different forms. One God. Three persons. Three in One.

Maybe you were named after a family member. Maybe you were named after a friend of your parents. Maybe you don't know who or what you were named after. But your name likely means a lot to you. In biblical times, however, names meant more than just honoring a family member or friend. They carried with them a message about who a person was and what he or she was meant to be and do as part of God's people.

It is no surprise that the name *Jesus* is a particularly precious and meaningful name for our Lord and Savior. It is His personal name. The Hebrew word *Yshua* means, literally, "Yahweh saves." It includes portions of the name God revealed to Moses in the burning bush, *Yahweh*, along with the Hebrew word meaning "to save." When put together, the word *Jesus* in the Hebrew language is the name *Joshua*. When brought into the Greek language, the word *Joshua* is written *Jesus* or *Ihsous*. The name *Jesus* was revealed to his earthly father, Joseph, in a dream, as recorded in Matthew 1:21: "You shall call His name

Jesus, for He will save His people from their sins." And so the name Jesus was given to the Son of God.

John writes, "We know that this [Jesus] is indeed the Savior of the world" (4:42). In Acts 4:12 we read, "There is salvation in no one else, for there is no other name under heaven given among men by which we must be saved."

> **NEED TO KNOW**
>
> **Christ**: Greek for "Messiah." The title for Jesus that identifies Him as the one set apart by God to fulfill the Old Testament prophecies of a Savior.

The Anointed One

The other word commonly used as a name for Jesus is actually not a name, but a title. It is *Christ* or in the Greek language, *Xristos*, which means, "the Anointed One." It comes from the Hebrew word for "the anointed one," which is *Mashiach,* and so in Greek, "Messiah." In the days of the Old Testament kings, the one who was anointed with oil by God's prophet was the one God had chosen to be king. The ancient tradition of anointing kings in the Western world with oil at their coronation derives from this ancient Jewish practice. Anointing was a common practice among God's people in the Old's Testament for setting apart priests, prophets, and kings for their service. Even to this day in some churches' rites of ordination, oil is applied to the one being ordained a minister in the church.

We read in Psalm 45:7, "God, your God, has anointed you with the oil of gladness beyond your companions." And in John 3:34, Jesus says of Himself, "He whom God has sent utters the words of God, for He gives the Spirit without measure." And then in Acts 10:38, Peter declares, "God anointed Jesus of Nazareth with the Holy Spirit and with power."

And so when we put the word *Christ* behind the name *Jesus*, we have the name *Jesus Christ.* It has become such a common phrase that many people assume that Jesus' name is simply Jesus Christ. But, in fact, what we are saying and confessing when we say "Jesus Christ" is simply this: "Jesus is the one sent by God to be the world's Savior."

The Name We Most Often Use Today: Jesus Christ

It is interesting to note that in the days of the early Lutheran Church, the use of the word *Jesus* was not quite as common as it is today, instead it was more common to refer to "the Lord Christ" and "Christ." Jesus was regarded as a very

MAKING CONNECTIONS

After the Reformation, Lutherans were sometimes made fun of by other Protestants because they would bow their heads reverently when saying the word *Jesus* in their prayers and in their worship services. They were simply continuing the ancient practice among Christians of expressing outward reverence when the name *Jesus* was spoken. It is a good and pious custom, and some may wish to either start or continue to do this.

special and holy name, and reverence was expressed when it was spoken.

Jesus Christ is the most common name we use for Jesus, but the Scriptures also use many other words as titles for Jesus, such as these:

"angel of God" (Exodus 14:19)
Redeemer (Isaiah 59:20)
Immanuel (Matthew 1:23)
Son of the living God (Matthew 16:16)
Son of Man (Matthew 25:31)
the Word (John 1:14)

Such titles for Jesus are simply ways that the meaning of His life and work are expressed. He **redeems** the world from sin, paying for our sins with His perfect life and innocent suffering and death. He is the **"angel" or "messenger" of God**. He is the very **Son of the living God** as the Second Person of the Holy Trinity. He is also the **Son of Man**, the ultimate firstborn of all creation, sent into our human flesh to save us. He is the **Word** of God, the ultimate and full revelation of who God is and what He means for us and does for us.

Jesus Christ Is Lord

Another common title used in connection with Jesus Christ is *Lord*. We often will read in the Scriptures the phrase, "the Lord Jesus Christ." (See Acts 11:17; Romans 1:7; 1 Corinthians 1:2.) The New Testament Scriptures, written in Greek, use the word *Kyrios* for "Lord." That word *Kyrios* carries with it tremendous meaning, particularly when applied to Jesus. Perhaps the most dramatic and powerful use of the word *Lord* to refer to Jesus is found in Philippians 2:11, where Paul writes, "Jesus Christ is Lord." To understand precisely what Paul means, we need to learn a bit about ancient Jewish ways of referring to God.

Because the name God revealed to Moses in Exodus 3 was regarded as so holy as to be unspeakable by human beings, it became the practice when the letters for the name *YHWH* were written to include little marks underneath the consonants to signal the reader to say the word *Adonai* or *Lord* rather than actually say out loud YHWH. Therefore, when the people of God heard the Scriptures read, they would hear "Lord" rather than Yahweh. And so, when Paul wrote, "Jesus Christ is Lord" he is saying much more than that Jesus Christ is over all things; he is asserting that Jesus Christ is none other than YHWH in the flesh.

This assertion would have shocked and amazed those who were familiar with the holy name of God, but it was no more shocking than what Jesus Himself did often in His ministry. Jesus once horrified the religious leaders listening to Him when He said of Himself, "Before Abraham was, I am" (John 8:58). He specifically used the holy name of God, the great "I AM," and told them that He, Jesus of Nazareth, was in fact the great Lord of lords and King of kings. What is more, Jesus uses the "I am" phrase to describe Himself and His work elsewhere in the New Testament. "I am the bread

NEED TO KNOW

Lord: from the Greek *Kyrios*, used with the name of Jesus to indicate that He is both Lord and God. Indicates He is true man and true God.

NEED TO KNOW

When Moses asked God to reveal His name, God said, "I AM WHO I AM" (Exodus 3:14). The Hebrew language uses only consonants יהוה, and so the name of God transliterated in four letters as *YHWH* and articulated as *Yahweh*. This four-letter representation of God's personal name is called the **tetragrammaton** from the Greek for "consisting of four letters."

of life" (John 6:35, 48, 51). "I am the light of the world" (John 8:12). "I am the door of the sheep" (John 10:7, 9). "I am the good shepherd" (John 10:11, 14). "I am the resurrection and the life" (John 11:25). "I am the true vine" (John 15:1, 5). And, as we have seen, "I am the way, and the truth, and the life" (John 14:6). For more on Jesus' "I AM" statements, see pages 54–57.

I Believe in Jesus Christ

So, what's in a name? Much indeed! We cherish the revealed names and titles for Jesus. We use them reverently and carefully when we pray, when we worship, and when we speak about Jesus. And it is precisely for this reason that we will take care never to use the word in a dishonorable way or to use it as a "swear word." Such uses ought to make us cringe with discomfort. The name is the name above every name (Philippians 2:9).

When we say, "I believe in Jesus Christ," we are saying we believe that Jesus, the son of Mary, the first-century Palestinian Jew from the town of Nazareth, is in fact our Savior from sin, death, and hell. He is none other than the Son of God, the Second Person of the Holy Trinity, sent into this world to fulfill for us perfectly the whole Law of God and then to offer up to His Father the once-for-all sacrifice for the sins of the world. This God-man's blood cleanses us from all sin. Believing this, we have life in His name. John says, "This is eternal life, that they know You, the only true God, and Jesus Christ whom You have sent" (17:3). And in John 3:36, Jesus tells us, "Whoever believes in the Son has eternal life; whoever does not obey the Son shall not see life, but the wrath of God remains on him." The apostle Paul tells Timothy, "I know whom I have believed, and I am convinced that He is able to guard until that day what has been entrusted to me" (2 Timothy 1:12). And in Romans, Paul writes, "For with the heart one believes and is justified, and with the mouth one confesses and is saved" (10:10).

Two Letters Make for a Huge Confession of Faith

The word *Christ* was also used in the "Chi-Rho," one of the Christian Church's most ancient symbols. It consists of the first two letters in the Greek word for *Christ*, the letters *Chi* (an X-shaped letter) and the letter *Rho* (a P-shaped letter). Hence, in ancient Christian places of worship, in Roman catacombs, and in other areas where Christians would gather for worship, it is common to find this symbol, and so also to this very day. You will commonly see the Chi-Rho symbol in stained glass, or inscribed on church altars and pulpits, or sewn onto the special clothing clergy wear. Sometimes we see the Chi-Rho used along with the Greek letters *Alpha* **A** and *Omega* **Ω**. *Alpha* is the first letter in the Greek alphabet; *Omega* is the last. In Revelation 22:13, Jesus says, "I am the Alpha and the Omega, the first and the last, the beginning and the end." Jesus both contains and encompasses all of reality, guiding and shaping all things for the salvation of mankind.

Study Questions

1. What is the Trinity? Why is the Trinity so central to Christianity?

2. In Old Testament times, what was the significance of being anointed with oil? How is this practice continued today?

3. Read Philippians 2:9–11. What is Paul really saying when He says "Jesus Christ is Lord"? Why would this have been shocking to the religious leaders with whom he was speaking?

4. List the various titles for Jesus you learned about in this chapter. How do these titles express the meaning of His life and work?

5. When you say, "I believe in Jesus Christ," what are you really saying?

Visit lutheranism101.com to download the free Leader Guide.

6. Draw the Chi-Rho, complete with the Greek letters that are often included with this symbol. Label each part and explain its meaning. As a whole, what is the significance of this symbol?

Discussion Questions

1. What is the meaning of your name? What importance does your name hold for you?

2. The name God revealed to Moses in Exodus 3:14 (I AM WHO I AM, transliterated as YHWH and articulated as *Yahweh*) was regarded as so holy that it could not be spoken by human beings. Yet, Jesus horrified the religious leaders listening to Him when He said of Himself, "Before Abraham was, I AM" (John 8:58). Jesus specifically used the holy name of God, the great "I AM" and told them that He, Jesus of Nazareth, was the great Lord of lords and King of kings. What other things or teachings did Jesus say during His earthly ministry that would horrify people today, perhaps even including some Christian leaders?

3. Read Exodus 20:1–7. What is the Second Commandment? Why do you think God made this commandment second only to "You shall have no other gods before Me"? (See *Luther's Small Catechism with Explanation* pp. 61–67 for an explanation of the Second Commandment.)

Visit lutheranism101.com to download the free Leader Guide.

CHAPTER 4

Prophet, Priest, and King: Jesus Is All Three

In This Chapter

- Jesus is a prophet sent to exhort you to turn from sin and pursue righteousness.
- Jesus is your High Priest and always lives to mediate between you and the Father.
- Jesus is still the King of kings and reigns over heaven and earth.

FROM THE BIBLE

Jesus was anointed (set apart) to be a prophet:

Moses said, "The Lord God will raise up for you a prophet like me from your brothers. You shall listen to Him in whatever He tells you" (Acts 3:22). God anointed Jesus of Nazareth with the Holy Spirit and with power. He went about doing good and healing all who were oppressed by the devil, for God was with Him (Acts 10:38).

In addition to the names and titles used for Jesus in the New Testament, we observe three distinct roles being fulfilled by Jesus, perfectly and completely fulfilled. Traditionally these are referred to as the offices of Christ: prophet, priest, and king. These roles are yet another helpful way for organizing and understanding what Scripture teaches about the work of Jesus for us and for our salvation.

Jesus Fulfills the Office of Prophet

What is a prophet? Most people think a prophet is somebody who tells the future. While there is truth to this, the biblical prophets were, most important of all, men who proclaimed God's truth by telling people what God wanted them to say. They were preachers of God's Word. Jesus is the last and final prophet because He personally preached during His life here on earth for three years. He continues to this day, through the Church's ministry, to proclaim the Good News of salvation. Jesus as prophet was promised to God's people centuries before He was ever born. Moses said in Deuteronomy 18:15, "The Lord your God will raise up for you a prophet like me from among you, from your brothers—it is to Him you shall listen." Both at Jesus' Baptism and at His transfiguration, God the Father said, "This is My beloved Son, with whom I am well pleased" (Matthew 3:17; 17:5), and at the transfiguration, He added, "Listen to Him."

To hear the words of Jesus is to hear the prophetic teachings of God's truth, and to these truths we cling for hope and salvation. Jesus' mission was, first and foremost, to preach and proclaim the Good News of salvation found in Him. John tells us, "The law was given through Moses, grace and truth came through Jesus Christ. No one has ever seen God; the only God, who is at the Father's side, He has made Him known" (John 1:17–18). Consider that passage carefully. "No one has ever seen God." Here we understand that "God" means "God the Father." "No one has ever seen" Him, except for the Son of God, the Second Person of the Trinity. His role as official teacher and preacher of God was fulfilled in the New Testament, but He also carried out this task throughout the Old Testament in all those instances when the "messenger of the Lord" appeared to reveal God's Word to various people at various times.

To Whom Shall We Go?

Peter summarized just how vital the prophetic office of Christ is when he told Jesus, "Lord, to whom shall we go? You have the words of eternal life" (John 6:68). Jesus, and Jesus alone, is our great prophet, the One through whom we can and do know God the Father's will, which is given as a gift to us through the work of God the Holy Spirit.

The prophetic work of Jesus continues to this very day as the Church's preaching office declares the truth of the Gospel: that Jesus is the Son of God and the world's Redeemer. Jesus commissioned His apostles to go into all the world and proclaim the Gospel (Mark 16:15). He told His apostles and consequently all pastors who faithfully preach the same message, "The one who hears you hears Me, and the one who rejects you rejects Me, and the one who rejects Me rejects Him who sent Me" (Luke 10:16). Christ's ministers stand in the great line of all faithful servants who carry out the prophetic office of Christ. Paul describes His work and all who share in it as that of being "ambassadors for Christ, God making His appeal through us. We implore you on behalf of Christ, be reconciled to God" (2 Corinthians 5:20).

Jesus Fulfills the Office of Priest

But Jesus is not only a preacher of truth and one through whom we have the full, final, complete, and wholly trustworthy Word of God. He is also our great and final High Priest. Through what we call His "active obedience" on our behalf, He kept all parts of God's Law, making up for our many and constant faults, failings, and sins. Paul says, "When the fullness of time had come, God sent forth His Son, born of woman, born under the law, to redeem those who were under the law, so that we might receive adoption as sons" (Galatians 4:4–5).

Throughout the Old Testament times, the priests of God offered daily sacrifices, all pointing to the Messiah's last and final sacrifice for all sins. The Book of Hebrews offers this beautiful explanation of how Jesus is our great High Priest and does the priestly work of offering the once-for-all sacrifice of Himself for our sins:

> The former priests were many in number, because they were prevented by death from continuing in office, but He holds His priesthood permanently, because He continues forever. Consequently, He is able to save to the uttermost those who draw near to God through Him, since He always lives to make intercession for them.
>
> For it was indeed fitting that we should have such a high priest, holy, innocent, unstained, separated from sinners, and exalted above the heavens. He has no need, like those high priests, to offer sacrifices daily, first for His own sins and then for those of the people, since He did this once for all when He offered up Himself. For the law appoints men in their weakness as high priests, but the word of the oath, which came later than the law, appoints a Son who has been made perfect forever. (7:23–28)

The Priest Who Sacrificed Himself

What, exactly, does the sacrifice of Jesus Christ for our sins accomplish? John writes, "He is the propitiation for our sins, and not for ours only but also for the sins of the whole world" (1 John 2:2). We need to pause here and talk about that unusual and perhaps unfamiliar word *propitiation*. To "propitiate" is to perform an action that appeases or satisfies an angry deity. That general meaning would have been familiar to the audience of the letters of John. But we need to go even more deeply to understand fully the impact of John's word. The Greek word that we translate as "propitiation" is the word *hilasmos*. Understanding the vocabulary used by John when he explains the work of Christ provides us with a rich discovery of Gospel treasure.

At the time of the first Christians, the Old Testament had been translated into Greek. This became the most commonly used form of the Old Testament by both the early Christian Church and much of Judaism at the time. Greek became the universal language of the known world as a result of the remarkable life of Alexander III of Macedon, commonly known as "Alexander the Great." He lived from 356 to 323 BC, and by age 30 he had conquered the known world in his time, from Greece all the way to India, bringing with him the Greek language and culture everywhere he went. Greek became such a dominant language that Jewish scholars worked on a translation of the entire Old Testament, which became known as the Septuagint. Greek remained the common language throughout the Roman Empire during the years of Christ and into the first several centuries of the Church's history.

The use of the word *hilasmos* would have made those hearing John's letter for the first time think of a passage from the Greek Old Testament in Exodus 25:17–18: "You shall make a mercy seat [*hilastérion*] of pure gold. Two cubits and a half shall be its length, and a cubit and a half its breadth. And you shall make two cherubim of gold; of hammered work shall you make them, on the two ends of the mercy seat."

TECHNICAL STUFF

Old Testament priests and sacrifices were imperfect, but Christ, His work, and His sacrifice were perfect. The **active obedience** of Christ consists in His substitutionary work of freeing us from the demands of the Law and obtaining perfect righteousness for us by perfectly fulfilling, as our Substitute, the entire Law in all its demands, so that His righteousness may be made our own by faith (Matthew 5:17; Romans 10:4: Galatians 4:4–5). His **passive obedience** consists in His substitutionary work of freeing us from the penalties provided by the Law for all sinners; He did this by taking our sins on Himself and suffering our punishment in our stead (Isaiah 53; Galatians 3:13; Ephesians 5:2; Colossians 1:14; 1 Peter 2:21–24; 1 John 1:7). —Adapted from O. C. J. Hoffmann, in "Office, or Work, of Christ," *The Abiding Word*, ed. T. Laetsch (St. Louis, 1947), 2:135–44.

The Ark of the Covenant: Powerful Witness to Salvation in Christ

This passage describes the ark of the covenant. The ark of the covenant contained sacred objects, including the original copy of the Ten Commandments as given to Moses. It was carried in solemn procession by the people of Israel during their forty years of wandering in the desert after being released from their slavery in Egypt. When the people rested, they put the ark of the covenant into the holiest part the tabernacle, the Most Holy Place. Later, when Solomon built the first permanent temple, the ark was moved into the Most Holy Place there. The entrance to the Most Holy Place was covered by a thick drape. Once a year, on the Jewish festival called the Day of Atonement, blood from a sacrifice was sprinkled on the Mercy Seat, signifying God's acceptance of that blood as payment for the sins of the people. It is explained by the apostle Paul in Romans:

> [Jesus,] whom God put forward as a propitiation [*hilastérion*] by His blood, to be received by faith. This was to show God's righteousness, because in His divine forbearance He had passed over former sins. (3:25)

> Above it were the cherubim of glory overshadowing the mercy seat [*hilastérion*]. Of these things we cannot now speak in detail. (Hebrews 9:5)

> He is the propitiation [*hilasmos*] for our sins, and not for ours only but also for the sins of the whole world. (1 John 2:2)

> In this is love, not that we have loved God but that He loved us and sent His Son to be the propitiation [*hilasmos*] for our sins. (1 John 4:10)

And so, when we read in the New Testament about Jesus being our "propitiation" (*hilasmos*), we are reading that Jesus is Himself the perfect atoning sacrifice—both the sacrifice and the last and final Mercy Seat—the "propitiation" for all our sins. Jesus continues His priestly work before the Father, praying constantly for His Church. He is, as John says, our "advocate with the Father" because He, and He alone, is the righteous and holy One (1 John 2:1).

The Ark, the Tabernacle, and the Temple

26.4 in wide
1.5 cubits
(Ex 37:1)

26.4 in high
1.5 cubits
(Ex 37:1)

44 in long
2.5 cubits
(Ex 37:1)

© Hugh Claycombe

THE TABERNACLE

The new religious observances taught by Moses in the desert centered on rituals connected with the tabernacle and amplified Israel's sense of separateness, purity, and oneness under the lordship of Yahweh.

A few desert shrines have been found in Sinai, notably at Serabit el-Khadem and at Timnah in the Negeb, and show marked Egyptian influence.

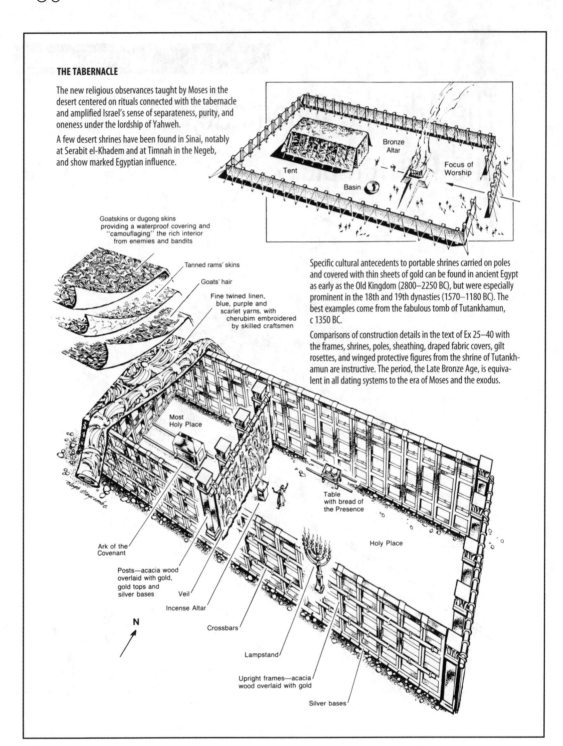

Specific cultural antecedents to portable shrines carried on poles and covered with thin sheets of gold can be found in ancient Egypt as early as the Old Kingdom (2800–2250 BC), but were especially prominent in the 18th and 19th dynasties (1570–1180 BC). The best examples come from the fabulous tomb of Tutankhamun, c 1350 BC.

Comparisons of construction details in the text of Ex 25–40 with the frames, shrines, poles, sheathing, draped fabric covers, gilt rosettes, and winged protective figures from the shrine of Tutankhamun are instructive. The period, the Late Bronze Age, is equivalent in all dating systems to the era of Moses and the exodus.

SOLOMON'S TEMPLE

960–587 BC

The temple of Solomon, located adjacent to the king's palace, functioned as God's royal palace and Israel's national center of worship. By its symbolism, the sanctuary taught the rule of the Lord over the whole creation and His special headship over Israel.

The floor plan is a type that has a long history in Semitic religion, particularly among the West Semites. An early example of the tripartite division into 'ulam, hekal, and debir (portico, main hall, and inner sanctuary) has been found at Syrian Ebla (c 2300 BC) and, much later but more contemporaneous with Solomon, at Tell Ta'yinat in the Orontes basin (c 900 BC). Like Solomon's, the latter temple has three divisions, contains two columns supporting the entrance, and is located adjacent to the royal palace.

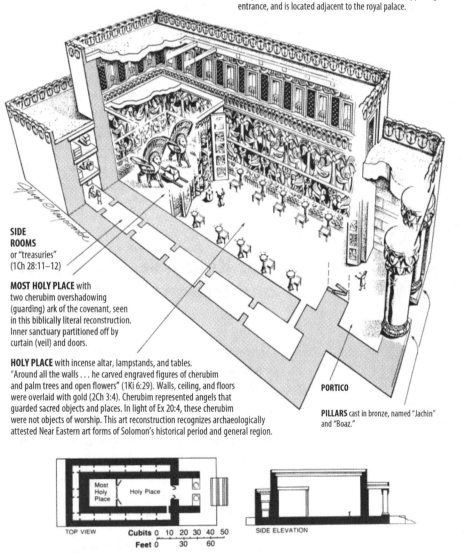

SIDE ROOMS or "treasuries" (1Ch 28:11–12)

MOST HOLY PLACE with two cherubim overshadowing (guarding) ark of the covenant, seen in this biblically literal reconstruction. Inner sanctuary partitioned off by curtain (veil) and doors.

HOLY PLACE with incense altar, lampstands, and tables. "Around all the walls . . . he carved engraved figures of cherubim and palm trees and open flowers" (1Ki 6:29). Walls, ceiling, and floors were overlaid with gold (2Ch 3:4). Cherubim represented angels that guarded sacred objects and places. In light of Ex 20:4, these cherubim were not objects of worship. This art reconstruction recognizes archaeologically attested Near Eastern art forms of Solomon's historical period and general region.

PORTICO

PILLARS cast in bronze, named "Jachin" and "Boaz."

Most Holy Place   Holy Place

TOP VIEW   Cubits 0 10 20 30 40 50
Feet 0   30   60

SIDE ELEVATION

BELIEVE, TEACH, CONFESS

Great and mighty Kings often serve only themselves, but our King, Jesus, is at work in us and through us to accomplish great and might things on our behalf. The Lutheran Confessions indicate that: "Good works are to be done because of God's command and for the exercise of faith—confessing the faith and giving thanks. Good works must be done for these reasons. They are done in the flesh, which is not as yet entirely renewed. The flesh hinders the Holy Spirit's motives and adds some of its uncleanness to the works. Yet, because of Christ, they are holy, divine works, sacrifices, and acts belonging to the rule of Christ, who in this way displays His kingdom before this world. For in these works He sanctifies hearts and represses the devil. In order to retain the Gospel among people, He openly sets the confession of saints against the kingdom of the devil and, in our weakness, declares His power." (Ap V 68)

Jesus Fulfills the Office of King

The third and final office of Christ we learn about from the Scriptures is His office as King. Earthly kings exercise great power and rule over their lands and people. Christ the King rules over all of creation. He says, "All authority in heaven and on earth has been given to Me" (Matthew 28:18). He spoke these words at His ascension and with them charged the apostles and all who follow in the Office of the Holy Ministry to go "and make disciples of all nations, baptizing them in the name of the Father and of the Son and of the Holy Spirit" (Matthew 28:19). Additionally, in the name of their King, all Christians have the duty and blessed opportunity to "proclaim the excellencies of Him who called you out of darkness into His marvelous light" (1 Peter 2:9).

Our King Rules through Word and Sacrament

As our King, Jesus guides, guards, and governs His Church through His Means of Grace, the Word and the Sacraments. It was tempting at the time of Christ for people to look to Him to be the "great problem solver" and to take care of every possible thing they needed or wanted in this temporal and transitory life. There were times when people wanted to make Him an earthly King, and His mission was constantly misunderstood, even by His closest followers. Time and again He had to correct these misunderstandings. He said during His trial before Pilate, "My kingdom is not of this world. If My kingdom were of this world, My servants would have been fighting, that I might not be delivered over to the Jews. But My kingdom is not of this world" (John 18:36). Pilate had been told that Jesus was a threat to his authority as the governor of the Roman province of Palestine and so was particularly eager to get to the bottom of precisely what Jesus said about Himself. Jesus acknowledges that He is a King, but unlike any Pilate or others expected or feared. He continued, "For this purpose, I was born and for this purpose I have come into the world—to bear witness to the truth. Everyone who is of the truth listens to My voice" (John 18:37).

Our King, Jesus, leads all of us to our heavenly home, to the glory that is yet to be revealed on the day of the great resurrection of all the dead. The Church in heaven is known as the kingdom of glory. Here on earth, we will have troubles. Christ told us this and cautions anyone who thinks that following Him is a way to avoid trouble, hardship, or persecution. He has cautioned us so we will not be surprised by this, but He offers this powerful comfort: "I have said these things to you, that in Me you may have peace. In the world you will have tribulation. But take heart; I have overcome the world" (John 16:33). Paul wrote what every Christian must hold to steadfastly until the end, finding hope in these assurances: "The Lord will rescue me from every evil deed and bring me safely into His heavenly kingdom. To Him be the glory forever and ever. Amen" (2 Timothy 4:18).

Jesus is our Prophet, Priest, and King. All glory be to Him!

The *I Am* Statements of Christ

Throughout the Old Testament, the most frequent name for God is "Yahweh," used more than 5,000 times. This Hebrew name for God comes from God Himself, as Moses records. When Moses asked God by what name He desired to be called, God replied, "I AM WHO I AM" (Exodus 3:14). When Moses began preaching to the Israelites, he explained to them, "'He Is' sent me." Or, literally in Hebrew, "Yahweh sent me."

The Gospel of St. John builds on this Old Testament event and this personal name for God in order to explain who Jesus is. The Jewish people of Jesus' day knew Moses' story about "I AM" and Moses' preaching in the name of "He Is." This name for God was so sacred that they would never utter it. In view of this background, imagine the outrage of the Pharisees when Jesus described Himself by repeatedly using the phrase "I am." Based on the Greek original, here are the places in John where Christ refers to Himself as "I am": 4:26; 6:20, 35, 41, 48, 51; 8:12, 24, 28, 58; 9:9; 10:7, 9, 11, 14; 11:25; 13:19; 14:6; 15:1, 5; 18:5–6, 8.

The following examples will explain Jesus' statements and help you better understand who Jesus is.

I Am the Bread of Life

John records various times when Christ described Himself as "I am" followed with a statement about bread. Christ refers to Himself as "the bread of life" (6:35, 48). He is "the bread that came down from heaven" (6:41) and "the living bread" (6:51). The Jews were stunned. "How can this man give us His flesh to eat?" Their grumbling leads Christ to add that He is "the bread that came down from heaven" (6:4).

In speaking these words, Christ drew a parallel between His life and the manna God provided during the exodus. Christ taught the Pharisees: "In the desert, God provided manna. This manna kept your ancestors alive; however, because of original sin, they eventually died. Like the manna God provided, I came from heaven, but I give eternal life" (John 6:32–33, paraphrase; cf. vv. 48–51; Psalm 78:23–33).

According to John, Christ's teaching on the bread of life was a pivotal point in His ministry. Because of Christ's words about eating and drinking His flesh and blood, many disciples "no longer walked with Him" (John 6:66). They found His teachings too difficult. Yes, just as food is necessary for earthly life, Christ is necessary for life eternal.

I Am the Light of the World

At the beginning of the Gospel, John called Christ "the light of men" (1:4). In 8:12, we learn where John first heard the term *light* used in reference to Christ. The term came from Christ Himself as He addressed the Pharisees in the temple court near the place where offerings were put (8:13, 20). Historically, the Pharisees were aware of the messianic prophecies about light found in passages such as Isaiah 42:6 and Daniel 2:22. Therefore, speaking in terms the Jews would understand, Christ witnessed that He fulfilled these prophecies. However, Christ does not stop there. He followed His words "I am the light" by quickly adding "of the world" (John 8:12). By adding this phrase, Christ testified that He is the fulfillment of God's plan for Jews and Gentiles alike (Isaiah 49:6).

The second mention of Jesus as the "light of the world" occurs in John 9:5. This teaching prepares people for the healing of a blind man. Again, it is addressed to the Pharisees. Soon after calling Himself "the light of the world," Christ offered proof of His power over blindness, fulfilling Isaiah 29:18; 35:5. Christ, the light of the world, brought light into the blind man's darkness.

Some scholars suggest that the blind man symbolized the Gentile nations, which received the light after the Jews rejected it. However, if symbolism is involved, it is most likely that the blind man symbolized all sinners, who languish in darkness until the light (Christ) shines in their lives. The brilliance of His glory will open your eyes!

I Am the Door

In ancient times, sheep were kept in walled enclosures with only one entrance. Jesus calls Himself the door (John 10:7, 9), for only through Him will true shepherds (pastors and other faithful witnesses) enter to guide the lost sheep. Christ addresses this teaching to the Pharisees. He accuses them of providing false witness. Christ provides the test for who is a true and faithful shepherd. True shepherds do not proclaim themselves, but the Lord. Christ alone provides our security.

I Am the Good Shepherd

The Pharisees knew the Old Testament passages in which humanity was called God's "sheep" and God their "shepherd" (Psalm 23:1). Therefore, in His first "I am the good shepherd" pronouncement, Christ tells the Pharisees that, unlike a hired hand who watches the sheep and runs at the slightest hint of danger, a good shepherd protects His sheep, even to the point of death (10:11).

In His second "I am the good shepherd" pronouncement, Christ spoke pointedly. He would die for His sheep; that includes you and me. John mentions that Christ spoke of "sheep that are not of this fold" (10:16). Those of Christ's fold are the Jews, while those "not of this fold" are the Gentiles. Christ aimed His words at the traditional Jewish notion that salvation was for Jews alone. Christ also takes aim at our self-righteousness. His words teach each generation of believers to follow the Good Shepherd instead of contenting themselves with the idea that they walk with the right sheep.

I Am the Resurrection and the Life

Jesus' last "I am" statement closes out the first part of John's Gospel, which describes His travels and ministry. Lazarus, a friend of Jesus, is gravely ill. Mary and Martha, Lazarus's two sisters, send word to Jesus. Yet, He purposely stays away from Lazarus for two days, during which time Lazarus dies. Jesus tells His disciples that Lazarus has fallen asleep and that He is going to awaken him (11:11).

As we look at Christ's words today, it seems obvious that He is speaking about raising Lazarus from the dead. However, the disciples do not understand Christ's words as "Lazarus is dead," but only as "Lazarus is sleeping" (John 11:12–13). At this point, according to John, Christ tells His disciples specifically that Lazarus is not asleep, but dead. Jesus arrives at the home of Mary and Martha after Lazarus has been dead four days, his body in decay (11:39).

Perhaps you are wondering why John is so precise about recording how long Lazarus was in the tomb and that his corpse was in decay. Medical techniques were not as sophisticated then as they are today, and it was possible for someone to have a seizure, be pronounced dead, be laid in a tomb, and then recover. John wants his readers to know Lazarus was indeed dead and decaying.

As is the custom today, friends and relatives were coming to Mary and Martha's home to offer their condolences. In ancient times, the mourning period would last an additional three days. As Jesus approaches, Martha goes to meet Him. She confesses her belief in Christ's God-given power. She knew Christ could heal the sick. However, she has no idea Christ could raise the dead. Then Christ utters the key words of our text: "I am the resurrection and the life. Whoever believes in Me, though he die, yet shall he live, and everyone who lives and believes in Me shall never die" (11:25–26). What a wonderful testimony Christ offers Martha, as if to say, "The Father and I are one. Death has no power over the believer. Martha, live by the Holy Spirit, that you may know that I bring eternal life. Physical death no longer holds Lazarus captive. I have broken death's hold." Does Martha believe Christ's words? He asks. Her confession gushes forth, "Yes, Lord; I believe that You are the Christ, the Son of God, who is coming into the world" (11:27).

Conclusion

Christ intended that His "I am" statements would lead others to faith. His prayer offered just before He raised Lazarus demonstrates this: "I said this on account of the people standing around, that they may believe that You [God] sent Me" (11:42).

For Jewish readers, John's Gospel emphasizes that Jesus is Yahweh, come down among men. For other readers, John emphasizes that the one true God created and sustains the physical universe. For you and all generations, John affirms that there is no other Savior. Jesus is our bread, light, door, shepherd, and life.

—From *TLSB*, pp. 1784–85

Study Questions

1. What is a prophet? Are there prophets among us today? Explain.

2. Jesus is the great High Priest. How does He differ from the Old Testament priests?

3. What are three main differences between Jesus, our King, and earthly kings? Looking at your list of differences, why do you think people wanted to make Jesus an earthly king? (See, for example, John 6:1–2, 10–15.)

4. What was the purpose of the mercy seat?

5. What was placed underneath the mercy seat? Why?

Visit lutheranism101.com to download the free Leader Guide.

Discussion Questions

1. Read Exodus 25:1–9. Why were the Israelites told to build the Tabernacle? Today, what do Christians have instead of the Tabernacle?

2. Christ cautions anyone who thinks that following Him is a way to avoid trouble, hardship, or persecution. What type of hardships do you face as a Christian?

3. Why is it imperative that Christian pastors and teachers faithfully preach the Word of God?

4. In Jesus' time, people wanted Him to be an earthly king, a powerful leader who had come to rescue them from oppressive leaders and corrupt and ineffective leadership. They often misunderstood His mission. Why is it important for Christians today to have a clear understanding of who Jesus is, especially when it comes to matters of church and state?

Visit lutheranism101.com to download the free Leader Guide.

PART TWO

What you'll learn about:

- Jesus is unique in that He has two natures. He is both God and man.
- As God, Jesus does things only God can do.
- To be our Savior, it is absolutely necessary that Jesus is both true God and true man.

Who Is That God-Man?

Superheroes—they seem to be everywhere: movies, graphic novels, streaming videos, and so on. They possess amazing powers yet are still human beings. Is that what Jesus is? A kind Superman figure who performs miracles? No, He is much more than that. In Part Two, we will dive more deeply into what the Bible teaches about the God-man, Jesus Christ.

CHAPTER 5

The Greatest Mystery and Miracle of the Christian Faith: The Two Natures in Christ

NEED TO KNOW

Incarnation:.
From the Latin, meaning "becoming flesh." The scriptural teaching that the eternal uncreated Son of God "became flesh," taking on a human body and soul as He was miraculously conceived in the womb of the Virgin Mary; His divine nature was united with His human nature in one divine person, Jesus Christ. He forever remains both true man and true God (John 1:14; Philippians 2:5–8).

In This Chapter
• Jesus is God in the flesh.
• The quality and qualifications of God.
• Why it's important that Jesus is a true human being like us.

What We Know

What Scripture teaches about the nature of Jesus Christ is summarized in Luther's explanation of the Apostles' Creed:

> I believe that Jesus Christ, true God, begotten of the Father from eternity, and also true man, born of the Virgin Mary, is my Lord. (Small Catechism, The Second Article)

We refer to this reality as the doctrine of the two natures in Christ. Jesus Christ is one person with two natures: divine and human. Paul writes about this, "Great indeed, we confess, is the mystery of godliness: He was manifested in the flesh, vindicated by the Spirit, seen by angels, proclaimed among the nations, believed on in the world, taken up in glory" (1 Timothy 3:16). It is thought by many Bible scholars that in this verse Paul is repeating an ancient Christian hymn.

Our "In the Flesh" God

We human beings, limited by our reason and intellect, have struggled and always will struggle to wrap our minds around this wonderful and amazing mystery of the faith. And here we should pause a moment and consider that word *mystery*. We are not using that word in the sense of something to be solved, to be investigated, like a crime, with a solution to be found. It is rather the Greek word *mysterion* that, when the Bible was translated into Latin, was rendered with the word *sacramentum* or *sacrament*. In the Roman world, a "sacrament" was a solemn oath or vow given to a god. Christians took this word into their vocabulary to refer to a sacred action that God was taking on our behalf and for us!

The "mystery" of the incarnation—the sacred action God took on our behalf—is that God sent His Son into human flesh to be among us, and most important, to be for us and for our salvation. Human reason cannot fathom how this can be, but we can give our joyful assent to this reality and confess it as our most precious truth and saving fact. What we can do is take a closer look at what the Holy Scriptures reveal about the two natures in the one person of Jesus Christ. Remember: two natures, one person! Through the centuries, the Church came to more fully appreciate and articulate the wonderful mystery of the incarnation and what it means for our salvation.

MAKING CONNECTIONS

In the early centuries of the Church, while all Christians believed that Jesus was indeed the Son of God, the exact nature of what "Son" meant was contested, together with the precise relationship of the "Father," "Son," and "Holy Spirit" referred to in the New Testament. Debate on this subject occurred during the first four centuries of Christianity. The larger factions involved in this debate were the Jewish Christians, Gnostics, followers of Arius of Alexandria, and adherents of Pope Alexander of Alexandria.

Eventually, the teaching of Alexander, Athanasius, and the other ancient Church Fathers prevailed on the relationship of the Son in the Godhead, and it was settled as orthodox teaching that the Son was consubstantial and coeternal with the Father. All divergent beliefs were defined as heresies. This included Docetism, Arianism, and Sabellianism.

The most widely accepted definitions of the incarnation and the nature of Jesus were made by the First Council of Nicaea in 325, the Council of Ephesus

continued on page 64

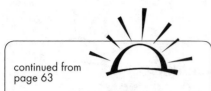

continued from page 63

in 431, and the Council of Chalcedon in 451. These councils declared that Jesus was both fully God, begotten from, but not created by the Father, and fully man, taking His flesh and human nature from the Virgin Mary. The human nature and divine nature are united into the one personhood of Jesus Christ.

TECHNICAL STUFF

Hypostatic union.

Theological term for the union of the two natures (divine and human) in the person of Jesus. They are separate yet act as a unit in the one person of Jesus. Jesus is God in flesh (John 1:1, 14; 10:30–33; 20:28; Philippians 2:5–8; Hebrews 1:8). He is fully God and fully man (Colossians 2:9). Therefore, there is a "union in one person of a full human nature and a full divine nature."

How Do We Know That Jesus Christ Is True God?

We know that Jesus is true God because He has divine names. Perhaps the most dramatic example of this can be found when the apostle Thomas saw the risen Lord Jesus for the first time. Have you heard the story of Thomas? The poor guy is forever known as "Doubting" Thomas, as if everyone else who encountered Jesus found it perfectly normal and natural that a person would come back from the dead after being so horribly tortured and then executed by crucifixion. Thomas, for some reason, was not with the rest of the apostles when Jesus first appeared among them that first Easter and said, "Peace be with you" (John 20:19). Imagine their mixed feelings of shock, fear, and joy when they saw their dear Master again! And so when they saw Thomas, they said, "We have seen the Lord." We can almost imagine Thomas just looking at them like they were all crazy and saying, "Right . . . sure you did." What we know he said was this: "Unless I see in His hands the mark of the nails, and place my finger into the mark of the nails, and place my hand into His side, I will never believe" (v. 25).

And so, eight days later, Jesus again appeared—only this time Thomas was there. Although the doors were securely locked, because the apostles were all terrified of being persecuted by the same crowds that had cheered on as Jesus was led away to be killed, Jesus suddenly appeared again among them, and again said, "Peace be with you" (John 20:26). And then Jesus made a point of saying to Thomas, "Put your finger here, and see My hands; and put out your hand, and place it in My side. Do not disbelieve, but believe" (v. 27).

There is nothing in the text to lead us to think that Thomas actually did what Jesus told him to do. No, instead, he simply burst out with one of the clearest confessions of the deity of Christ (v. 28): "My Lord and my God!"

A Shocking Statement: Jesus Is God

We need to understand what an astounding statement that was for a first-century faithful Jew to make. All their lives, as is the case with all the apostles, Jewish people would have repeated every morning and every evening as part of their daily prayers the great "Shemah," which is the first word in the Old Testament confession of faith in the one, true God: "Hear, O Israel! YHWH is our God, the Lord is One." This statement was made in the morning and in the evening, every single day, in a Jew's prayers. It was taught from early childhood and was supposed to be the very last thing on his or her lips at death: "Yahweh is our God! The Lord is One!" (Deuteronomy 6:4, author's translation).

שְׁמַע יִשְׂרָאֵל יְהוָה אֱלֹהֵינוּ יְהוָה| אֶחָד

Sh'ma Yisra'eil Adonai Eloheinu Adonai echad.

Hear, Israel, the Lord is our God, the Lord is One.

MAKING CONNECTIONS

Poor Thomas . . . always and forever he will be known as "Doubting" Thomas. But is he any different than us? No, not at all. We all want proof. While it would be wonderful to have Jesus show up and show us personally His wounded hands, feet, and side, the reality is that if there was a way to doubt the proof of the resurrection, we would. If we claimed to see someone resurrected from the dead today, we would hear, "You are delusional." We might be diagnosed with some kind of mental and emotional disturbance. Where can we find the "proof" we need today of Jesus? It's there every single time we gather around the Word of God with fellow believers. He's with us each time we receive our Lord's body and blood under the elements of bread and wine in the Lord's Supper. The Holy Spirit is working powerfully through these simple Means of Grace to call, to gather, and to shine the saving light of Christ into every dark nook and cranny of disbelief, sin, doubt, fear, and confusion in our lives.

What's in a Name?

Throughout Scripture, God uses a variety of names to reveal various aspects of Himself to us. Let's take a look at some of them and what they mean.

NAMES REVEALED IN THE OLD TESTAMENT IN HEBREW

> *Elohim,* deriving from the most ancient form of the Hebrew word for "God," which is "El." When used of the one true God, it means "the strong one." It is in the form of a plural word denoting the Trinity: that God is three in One. See Genesis 1:1; Deuteronomy 5:23; 8:15; Psalm 68:7; Isaiah 45:18; 54:5.

> *El Elyon,* meaning "the Most High God" emphasizing God's strength and supremacy above all things. See Genesis 14:19; Psalm 9:2; Daniel 7:18, 22, 25.

> *El Olam,* "the Everlasting God." This underscores the fact that God is unchanging and is a constant and inexhaustible source of love, kindness, and forgiveness. See Genesis 16:13.

> *Yahweh Tsidkenu,* often the name "YHWH" is used with other Hebrew words, and this example is particularly important: "The Lord our Righteousness." See Jeremiah 23:6.

NAMES REVEALED IN THE NEW TESTAMENT IN GREEK

> *Theos,* the generic Greek word for "God." This is the main word used in the New Testament for God. It teaches there is only one true God; He is utterly unique, transcendent, and our Savior. The word is used of Christ in verses such as John 1:1, 18, 20, 29; 1 John 5:20; Titus 2:13.

> *Despotes,* meaning "master." It conveys the idea of ownership; see Luke 2:29; Acts 4:24; 2 Peter 2:1; Jude 4; Revelation 6:10.

> *Pater,* meaning "Father." This is a unique New Testament revelation that comes only through faith in Christ. God becomes our own personal Father. Father is used of God in the Old Testament only 15 times, but in the New Testament, God is said to be "Father" more than 245 times. Jesus teaches us to call God "Father" in the Lord's Prayer.

Once again, however, let's remind ourselves that observant pious Jews never spoke the actual name of the Lord: *YHWH*. Instead they would say the Hebrew word for *Lord*, which is *Adonai*. When the Hebrew Bible was translated into Greek, the Greek word for *Lord*, *Kyrios*, was used to translate the word *Adonai*. Now we realize exactly how astounding was the confession Thomas made! He basically applied the great Shemah to Jesus! "My ADONAI, and my GOD!" He called Jesus YHWH and God. I wonder what was more shocking at that moment to those watching and hearing this—the fact that Jesus had appeared again or that Thomas had just uttered words that were nearly the same as the holy confession of Judaism about the Lord God Almighty!

Because the Bible Tells Us So

And so, without question, the New Testament writers do not say that Jesus was simply "divinely inspired" or acted in a "godly manner" or that He was a very religious person. No! The Scriptures teach us that Jesus is truly God. Let's turn now to another amazing example of the Bible's teaching that Jesus is God.

TECHNICAL STUFF

"Blasphemy" is a word that is now the stuff of punch lines in popular culture, so far removed are we from understanding what a very grave sin it is. The word *blasphemy* came into English from the Latin language, which in turned borrowed it from the Greek word *blasphemia,* which means "to slander." Therefore, to commit blasphemy is to lie about the most important thing in the world: God and His Word. When we misuse the name of God, we are using that holy name in a way that is deceptive.

In Romans 9:5, the apostle Paul writes that Jesus is from the Jewish race "according to the flesh" but is "the Christ who is God over all, blessed forever." This is another assertion that in the ears of the typical pious Jew would have been highly offensive, blasphemous, shocking, and amazing! Anyone saying such a thing about a mere man would deserve to be stoned to death for blasphemy.

Paul's words echo the classic prayer form that was used continually by the Jewish people whenever they prayed, the "Barukah." Here is a typical example of part of the prayers said before a meal:

> Blessed are You, O Lord our God, King of the universe, Who brings forth bread from the earth.

Again, the word for *Lord* said here is a substitute word for the name of God, *Yahweh*. And so when you read Paul's description of Jesus, that He is "God over all" and "blessed forever," you hear the echo of this sacred prayer form used by the Jews. What blasphemy it would be in the ears of the pious and devout Jews, such as Paul was before His conversion. What a powerful testimony to the divine nature of Christ!

TECHNICAL STUFF

The ***Communicatio Idiomatum***. Latin for "communication of properties." This is the teaching that the attributes of both the divine and human natures are ascribed to the one person of Jesus. This means that the man Jesus could lay claim to the glory He had with the Father before the world was made (John 17:5), claim that He descended from heaven (John 3:13), and also claim omnipresence (Matthew 28:20). All of these are divine qualities that are laid claim to by Jesus; therefore, the attributes of the divine properties were claimed by the person of Jesus.

And finally, one more example from the Scriptures where Jesus is referred to as God, this one from 1 John 5:20: "He [Jesus] is the true God and eternal life." Not "a" true God, or not "truly godly" but "He is the true God and eternal life." In each example we have mentioned, Jesus is not being given an "honorary title." The Scriptures cited are revealing precisely who and what Jesus is. He is the one and only true God.

Meeting the Qualifications to Be God

Jesus not only receives the title of "God," but He also exhibits the qualities and characteristics reserved only for God. Let's look at some examples of this.

God is **eternal**, that is, without beginning and end. "In the beginning was the Word and the Word was with God, and the Word was God. He was in the beginning with God" (John 1:1–2). Note carefully here that it does not say that the "Word was 'a' God." No, the Word was God.

God is **unchanging**. "Jesus Christ is the same yesterday and today and forever" (Hebrews 13:8).

God is **all-powerful** (omnipotence). Jesus says, "All authority in heaven and on earth has been given to Me" (Matthew 28:18).

God knows **everything** (omniscience). "Lord, You know everything" (John 21:17).

God is **present everywhere** (omnipresence). Jesus says, "Behold, I am with you always, to the end of the age" (Matthew 28:20).

Doing Things Only God Can Do: The Miracles of Jesus

Consider also the miracles of Jesus. That word *miracle* in the English is how we translate the Greek word *sign*. Miracles are "signs" of something about Jesus; the miracles of Jesus are dramatic testimonies that Jesus is God. Consider, for example, the miracle of how Jesus gave people food when they needed it (Luke 5:4–6), and then recall how God gave His people food to eat when they were wandering in the wilderness (Exodus 16). Another revealing incident occurs when Jesus calls Philip and Nathanael to follow Him. Without ever having met Nathanael, Jesus knows his name and everything about him (John 1:48). And think of the time Jesus met a woman at a well and knew things about her that she wanted to hide, but He, knowing all things, is able to diagnose her spiritual condition instantly (John 4:17–18).

We have seen that Jesus has divine names and possesses divine attributes. Now let's take note of how Jesus does things only God can and does do. First, and foremost, Jesus forgives sins. And nothing outraged the people of His day, who did not see in Him the promised Messiah, than His claim to be able to forgive sins. Ironically, their accusations against Jesus are poignant testimonies precisely to the fact that Jesus is God.

NEED TO KNOW

"It's a miracle!" We hear that so often it has almost lost its meaning. Anything that is amazing and wonderful or surprising or unexpected is said to be a "miracle." What actually is a miracle? Tracing the roots of the word is helpful. *Miracle* comes into English from the Latin *mirus*, which means "wonderful." And, of course, "full of wonder" is how everyone was left when they witnessed a miracle of Jesus! Why? Because a miracle was something so utterly unexpected and out of the ordinary and a cessation of the normal way of nature that it signaled that Jesus was something quite unique. In the New Testament, the "miracles" are often called "signs."

The Miracles of Jesus

		Matthew	Mark	Luke	John
1.	Water made into wine (Cana)				2:1–11
2.	Healing of an official's son (Cana)				4:46–54
3.	Healing of a man at the Pool of Bethesda (Jerusalem)				5:2–13
4.	Miraculous catch of fish (Lake of Gennesaret)			5:1–11	
5.	Healing of a man with an unclean spirit (Capernaum)		1:21–28	4:31–37	
6.	Healing of Peter's mother-in-law (Capernaum)	8:14–15	1:29–31	4:38–39	
7.	Healing of a leper (Galilee)	8:2–4	1:40–45	5:12–15	
8.	Healing of a paralytic (Capernaum)	9:2–8	2:1–12	5:17–26	
9.	Healing of a man with a withered hand (Galilee)	12:9–14	3:1–6	6:6–11	
10.	Healing of a centurion's servant (Capernaum)	8:5–13		7:1–10	
11.	Raising of a widow's son (Nain)			7:11–17	
12.	Healing of a blind and mute demon-oppressed man (Galilee)	12:22–28			
13.	Calming of a storm (Sea of Galilee)	8:23–27	4:35–41	8:22–25	
14.	Healing of two men with demons (Gadarenes)	8:28–34	5:1–20	8:26–39	
15.	Raising of Jairus's daughter (Capernaum)	9:18–26	5:22–43	8:41–56	
16.	Healing of a woman with a discharge of blood (Capernaum)	9:20–22	5:24–34	8:43–48	
17.	Healing of two blind men (at or near Capernaum)	9:27–31			
18.	Healing of a mute, demon-oppressed man (at or near Capernaum)	9:32–34			
19.	Feeding of the 5,000 (Bethsaida)	14:15–21	6:35–44	9:12–17	6:5–13
20.	Walking on water (Sea of Galilee)	14:24–34	6:47–53		6:16–21
21.	Healing of the daughter of a Canaanite woman (district of Tyre)	15:21–28	7:24–30		
22.	Healing of a deaf man with a speech impediment (Decapolis)		7:32–37		
23.	Feeding of the 4,000 (Decapolis)	15:32–38	8:1–9		
24.	Healing of a blind man (near Bethsaida)		8:22–26		
25.	Healing of a boy with an unclean spirit (near Mount of Transfiguration)	17:14–18	9:14–27	9:37–43	
26.	Provision of a shekel (Capernaum)	17:24–27			
27.	Healing of a blind man (Jerusalem)				9:1–41
28.	Healing of a mute man with a demon (Perea)			11:14–20	
29.	Healing of a woman with a disabling spirit (Perea or Judea)			13:10–17	
30.	Healing of a man with dropsy (Perea)			14:1–6	
31.	Raising of Lazarus (Bethany)				11:1–46
32.	Cleansing of ten lepers (border of Samaria and Galilee)			17:12–19	
33.	Healing of blind Bartimaeus and companion (Jericho)	20:29–34	10:46–52	18:35–43	
34.	Cursing of fig tree (near Jerusalem)	21:18–20	11:12–14, 20–25		
35.	Healing of Malchus's ear (Gethsemane)			22:49–51	18:10–11
36.	Second catch of fish (Sea of Tiberias)				21:1–14

—From *The Lutheran Study Bible*, p. 1596

Besides this list on the previous page, Jesus performed numerous miracles that the evangelists mention but do not describe (e.g., Matthew 4:23; 9:35; 11:21; Mark 6:56; Luke 4:40; 5:15; 6:17–18; 7:21; 10:13; John 2:23; 3:2; 4:45; 20:30; 21:25).

In Matthew 8, we read about a series of miracles Jesus did. He healed many people, such as a leper and a paralyzed man. He calmed a storm. He drove the devil out of two possessed men and into a herd of pigs, who then proceeded to stampede into the lake and drown. It was quite an eventful few days, culminating with the sad note in Matthew 8:34, "And behold, all the city came out to meet Jesus, and when they saw Him, they begged Him to leave their region." The people in the area were more concerned by the fact they had lost their pigs than that they had just witnessed an incredible miracle. And so Jesus did. He left them. He never forces Himself on anyone. It is possible to reject Jesus, but what a horrible and tragic decision that is!

The Greatest God-Thing Jesus Does: Forgive Sins

Matthew 9 tells us that Jesus crossed a lake and went to His own town again. Some people brought to Him a paralyzed man. After all, they had heard tales of this "miracle worker." Certainly, Jesus could help this man. What do you think they were expecting Him to do? Heal him! But what does Jesus do first? Forgive him! Jesus says, "Take heart, My son; your sins are forgiven" (Matthew 9:2). The religious authorities accused Jesus of being blasphemous

BELIEVE, TEACH, CONFESS

He did all His miracles by the power of this personal union. He showed His divine majesty, according to His pleasure, when and as He willed. He did this not just after His resurrection and ascension, but also in His state of humiliation. For example:

(a) At the wedding at Cana of Galilee [John 2:1–11]

(b) When He was twelve years old, among the learned [Luke 2:42–50]

(c) In the garden, when with a word He cast His enemies to the ground [John 18:6]

(d) In death, when He died not simply as any other man, but in and with His death conquered sin, death, devil, hell, and eternal damnation [Colossians 2:13–15]

The human nature alone would not have been able to do these miracles if it had not been personally united and had communion with the divine nature. (FC SD VIII 25)

WHAT DOES THIS MEAN?

When we ask God, "forgive us our trespasses," why do we ask and what does it mean? "We pray in this petition that our Father in heaven would not look at our sins, or deny our prayer because of them. We are neither worthy of the things for which we pray, nor have we deserved them, but we ask that He would give them all to us by grace, for we daily sin much and surely deserve nothing but punishment. So we too will sincerely forgive and gladly do good to those who sin against us." (Small Catechism, The Lord's Prayer, Fifth Petition)

because only God forgives sin. Who does Jesus think He is anyway?

"But Jesus, knowing their thoughts, said, 'Why do you think evil in your hearts?'" We see here once again in Jesus the divine attribute of omniscience, that He knows everything. And then He says, "For which is easier, to say, 'Your sins are forgiven,' or to say, 'Rise and walk'?" (Matthew 9:4–5).

Wow, that's a good question, Jesus! Consider this for a moment. What do you think? What's easier to say: "Your sins are forgiven" or "Get up and walk"? Well, frankly, it may have appeared to be easier to say, "Your sins are forgiven." After all, they are just words, right? Sure, they may be blasphemous, but words are just words. Any crazy man can say, "Your sins are forgiven." But if Jesus said, "Get up and walk" and the man did not, He would have exposed Himself as the fraud that they thought He was. So, what did Jesus do? He says, " 'But that you may know that the Son of Man has authority on earth to forgive sins'—He then said to the paralytic—'Rise, pick up your bed and go home'" (Matthew 9:6). You can almost hear the crowd that has gathered gasping in fear and awe at what happens next: "And he rose and went home. When the crowds saw it, they were afraid, and they glorified God, who had given such authority to men" (v. 7). And so here we see that because Jesus, true man, has the power to make the paralyzed man walk again, He has the power that God alone has: to forgive sins.

Creating, Judging, Receiving Honor and Glory: More God Things

What are other divine works Jesus has done? Consider this one: He is the Creator of all things! "All things were made through Him, and without Him was not any thing made that was made" (John 1:3). And in Colossians, Paul writes, "For by Him all things were created, in heaven and on earth, visible and invisible, whether thrones or dominions or rulers or authorities—all things were created through Him and for Him" (Colossians 1:16).

Jesus is also given the power to judge, "[The Father] has given Him authority to execute judgment" (John 5:27), and Jesus preserves all things in the universe, "He upholds the universe by the word of His power" (Hebrews 1:3).

Now let's consider events in Christ's ministry that demonstrate His divine power and authority. At the wedding in Cana, Jesus reveals His glory by turning real water into real wine (John 2:1–11). He rebukes and calms a violent storm (Luke 8:22–25). He heals many people of a wide range of sicknesses. He raises dead people to life, such as Lazarus (John 11:38–44). And finally He, Himself, rises from the dead (Matthew 28:6–7).

Another way we know Jesus is true God is the fact that the Bible records Jesus receiving the honor and glory that are reserved only for God. Jesus talks about this in John 5:22–23: "The Father judges no one, but has given all judgment to the Son, that all may honor the Son, just as they honor the Father. Whoever does not honor the Son does not honor the Father who sent Him." And in Hebrews 1:6, we read, "Let all God's angels worship Him.

MAKING CONNECTIONS
The Scandal of Forgiveness Today

When our pastors pronounce the Absolution in our worship services, many non-Lutherans are sometimes deeply offended and horrified and say the very same thing people in Jesus day said about Jesus: "Only God can forgive sins! Who does that guy think that he is?"

But listen very carefully to what your pastor is saying: "I, by virtue of my office, as a called and ordained servant of the Word, announce the grace of God unto all of you, and in the stead and by the command of my Lord Jesus Christ I forgive you all of your sins" (*LSB*, p. 185). Yes, Jesus is true God. He forgives sins and He does give such authority to men to do the same, in His name, according to His promise.

TECHNICAL STUFF

In 1 Peter 3:21, we hear that Baptism is an antitype. The words *type* and *antitype* are used in the Bible to refer to events, people, and objects in the Old Testament that have a fuller and clearer expression in the New Testament. What happens in the Old Testament is the type, and what happens in the New Testament is the antitype. In this passage, God's act of saving Noah and his family is the type, and God's act of saving us through Baptism is the antitype.

No better example of Jesus receiving divine honor and glory can be found in the entire New Testament than what Paul says about Him in Philippians 2:10, "At the name of Jesus every knee should bow, in heaven and on earth and under the earth, and every tongue confess that Jesus Christ is Lord, to the glory of God the Father." Paul chooses his words carefully, by the inspiration of the Holy Spirit. He is hearkening back to what we have mentioned before. The Jews never spoke the actual holy name of God out loud and instead would substitute the Hebrew word *Adonai* for the name *Yahweh* wherever it appeared in the text of the Old Testament. They even used the marks for the vowels in the word *Adonai* under the letters for *YHWH*. *Adonai* means "Lord." When the Old Testament was translated into Greek, the Greek word *Kyrios* was used for the Hebrew word *Adonai*. So now we can recognize the full impact of what Paul means when he writes, "And every tongue confess that Jesus Christ is Lord, to the glory of God the Father." Paul is declaring Jesus Christ to be Yahweh in the flesh!

Christians confess that Jesus Christ has two natures: God and man. He is not half God and half man. He is 100 percent God and 100 percent man. He never lost His divinity. He continued to exist as God when He became a man and added human nature to Himself (Philippians 2:5–11). Two historical heresies concerning Jesus' two natures are **Eutychianism** that claimed that His two natures are "mixed together" and **Monophysitism** that taught that in the person of Jesus, the two natures are combined into a new God-man nature.

Truly Man: A Male Human Being

If the Scriptures teach us that Jesus is truly God, how can He also be a true man? First, because the Scriptures clearly call Him "man." Note that when we refer to Jesus' human nature, we must be aware that Jesus is not merely "human" but is actually a real man, a male who was born of the Virgin Mary and lived and died as a true, actual male human being. Be careful about language that tries to avoid using male pronouns to refer to Jesus, or even God. We must stick with what has been revealed. And so we do not shy away from the reality that Jesus of Nazareth, a first-century Palestinian Jewish man, was true God and true man.

Paul clearly calls Jesus a man, "There is one God, and there is one mediator between God and men, the man Christ Jesus" (1 Timothy 2:5). Could it be any clearer than this? Scripture makes it clear that Jesus has a real human body and soul. On the night of His arrest before His crucifixion, Jesus said, "My soul is very sorrowful, even to death" (Matthew 26:38). In Luke 24:39, after His resurrection, Jesus had to show His disciples that they were not just imagining things: "See My hands and My feet, that it is I Myself. Touch Me, and see. For a spirit does not have flesh and bones as you see that I have."

Elsewhere, Scripture speaks about Jesus' real human feelings, sinless but very much real all the same. Jesus hungered (Matthew 4:2). Jesus wept (John 11:35). Jesus was thirsty (John 19:28). Jesus suffered and died (Matthew 26–27). Jesus was sleepy (Mark 4:38). And in one of the most beautiful explanations of why and how it is so comforting to know that Jesus was very much a real human being, we read the following in Hebrews 4:14–16:

> Since then we have a great high priest who has passed through the heavens, Jesus, the Son of God, let us hold fast our confession. For we do not have a high priest who is unable to sympathize with our weaknesses, but one who in every respect has been tempted as we are, yet without sin. Let us then with confidence draw near to the throne of grace, that we may receive mercy and find grace to help in time of need.

NEED TO KNOW

It has become common to avoid referring to a person's sex or "gender" when writing about men and women, or simply referring to mankind as a whole, er, excuse me, "humankind." There is nothing necessarily wrong with this, but it becomes very wrong when we see this happening with references to Christ. We should never avoid clear references to Christ's maleness. It is wrong to think that there is something like a generic human being, without sex and to never refer to a person's gender. "Male and female" He created mankind (Genesis 1:27). The Bible is very specific about the promise of a coming male born to a virgin woman (Isaiah 7:14), and we know this to be the Son of Mary, the Son of God, Jesus of Nazareth. Just take care not to let the politically correct atmosphere with language take away from the biblical truth of the one man, Jesus Christ, who suffered and died as a result of the sin of the one man, Adam.

MAKING CONNECTIONS

In the one Christ, we have the completely familiar, human flesh and bone, while at the same moment we have in our hands the eternal God. The disciples capture this wonder in the boat following Jesus' calming of the storm. They say, "Who then is this, that even wind and sea obey him?" (Mark 4:41). They questioned a sleeping carpenter and woke the mighty God. Here is a man of an altogether divine power. It is the combination of His nearness and His divine difference that overwhelms them. —Daniel Paavola, *Our Way Home: A Journey Through the Lord's Prayer* (St. Louis: Concordia, 2017)

NEED TO KNOW
Grace

Grace is a lovely word, often even a lovely name for a woman or girl. But what is "grace"? It is a word that in a biblical sense is somewhat unique. When we refer to a graceful performance by an artist, we are thinking of something beautiful and well done, but when the Bible uses that word, which in Greek is **charis**, it is referring to an undeserved free gift from God. Grace describes the work of the Holy Spirit in the hearts, minds, and lives of believers. The concept of grace is not just some abstraction, but, most important, denotes God's work of salvation among us. You may have seen this acrostic using the word *grace*: **G**od's **R**iches **a**t **C**hrist's **E**xpense. That's a nice little summary of it!

What a powerful thing it is to realize that because the Son of God is also very much a true man in the person of Jesus Christ He does sympathize with our weaknesses. He knows and understands what it means to be tempted, yet He overcame every temptation, where we so often fail. His victory over temptations and sin was on our behalf, and by grace, through faith, God applies the righteousness of Christ to us. As a result of all this, we are urged to come before the throne of grace with confidence. This is not a confidence derived from our own powers or work, but all because of Christ and His perfect righteousness. And in so doing we will indeed find the grace we need at all times and in every need.

Study Questions

1. People often struggle in their attempt to explain the mysteries of the Christian faith, including the two natures in Christ. What comes to mind when you hear the phrase *mystery of the faith*?

2. When the Bible was translated from Greek to Latin, the Greek word for *mystery* was rendered with the Latin word *sacramentum*. In the Roman world, what did this Latin word mean?

3. How does the meaning of this Latin word change the way you think about the phrase *mystery of the faith*?

4. What was Thomas's reaction when he finally saw the risen Lord with his own eyes? Why was his response so shocking to the other Jews standing around him?

5. Jesus is both true God and true Man. Fill out the chart using what you've learned in this chapter.

Qualities & Characteristics of God	Things Only God Can Do	Jesus' Human Qualities

Visit lutheranism101.com to download the free Leader Guide.

Discussion Questions

1. What does the word *blasphemy* mean? What are some examples of blasphemy that are common in our culture today?

2. Upon meeting the woman at the well, Jesus instantly diagnosed her spiritual condition (John 4:17–18). If Jesus were to meet you at the well, what do you think He would say?

3. If only God has the power to forgive sins, then what are you doing when you forgive others?

CHAPTER 6

The Essential Nature of Jesus' Two Natures

BELIEVE, TEACH, CONFESS

Jesus Is True Man

Here is how the foundational Lutheran confession of faith explains this wonderful truth about the incarnation: "Our churches teach that the Word, that is, the Son of God [John 1:14], assumed the human nature in the womb of the Blessed Virgin Mary. So there are two natures—the divine and the human—inseparably joined in one person. There is one Christ, true God and true man, who was born of the Virgin Mary, truly suffered, was crucified, died, and was buried. He did this to reconcile the Father to us and to be a sacrifice, not only for original guilt, but also for all actual sins of mankind [John 1:29].

"He also descended into hell, and truly rose again on the third day. Afterward, He ascended into heaven to sit at the right hand of the Father. There He forever reigns and has dominion over all creatures. He sanctifies those who believe in Him, by sending the Holy Spirit into their hearts to rule, comfort, and make them alive. He defends them against the devil and the power of sin.

"The same Christ will openly come again to judge the living and the dead, and so forth, according to the Apostles' Creed." (AC III 1–6)

In This Chapter

• What's the point of Jesus being true God and true man?

• Discover the power of Jesus' blood.

• When they get it wrong about Jesus' two natures.

So, we have established that the Scriptures teach that our Savior is both true God and true man. Why is it so important to keep these truths clear? Does it matter? Isn't this just another debate amongst theologians? No! The reality of our Lord's two natures is absolutely essential to understanding and praising God for the great work of salvation that the God-man Jesus Christ has accomplished for us.

Why Did God Have to Become Man?

Why did Jesus have to be a true man to be our Savior? First, so that He could stand in our place, fulfilling everything as a true human being that we could not, such as keeping God's Law perfectly. We refer to His fulfilling of the Law for us as His active obedience. Every tiny bit of God's Law is fulfilled entirely in Jesus Christ, for you and for me. As St. Paul says, "When the fullness of time had come, God sent forth His Son, born of woman, born under the law, to redeem those who were under the law, so that we might receive adoption as sons" (Galatians 4:4–5). And in Romans 5:19, we read, "For as by one man's disobedience the many were made sinners, so by the one man's obedience the many will be made righteous."

Secondly, Jesus had to be an actual and true human being in order to suffer and to die for our guilt of failing to keep God's Law perfectly. We refer to this as Christ's passive obedience. The prophet Isaiah writes in Isaiah 53 that like a lamb led to slaughter, Jesus suffered the punishment and penalty for sin that we deserve as a result of our sin. Paul says in Colossians 1:22, "He has now reconciled you in His body of flesh by His death, in order to present you holy and blameless and above reproach before Him." And Hebrews 2:14 says, "Since therefore the children share in flesh and blood, He Himself likewise partook of the same things, that through death He might destroy the one who has the power of death, that is, the devil."

Why Did Jesus Need to Be True God?

WHAT DOES THIS MEAN?
Jesus Is True God

It would be nearly impossible to find a more beautiful, clear, short explanation of the atoning sacrifice of Christ than what Luther wrote in the Small Catechism explaining the Second Article of the Apostles' Creed: "I believe that Jesus Christ, true God, begotten of the Father from eternity, and also true man, born of the Virgin Mary, is my Lord, who has redeemed me, a lost and condemned person, purchased and won me from all sins, from death, and from the power of the devil; not with gold or silver, but with His holy, precious blood and with His innocent suffering and death, that I may be His own and live under Him in His kingdom and serve Him in everlasting righteousness, innocence, and blessedness, just as He is risen from the dead, lives and reigns to all eternity. This is most certainly true."

We see how Jesus had to be true man, but why true God? Why not just have an ordinary man appointed to the task of saving the world, a kind of "superman" heroic figure? Again, Scripture provides our answers.

Christ had to be true God so that His fulfilling of the Law would be a sufficient ransom for all people. No mere man could accomplish such a thing, but only

MAKING CONNECTIONS

Have you ever wondered what the great "Indulgence controversy" was all about? In the Middle Ages, the Roman Church allowed, encouraged, and eagerly wanted people to believe that by performing an act of penance or paying for an "indulgence" on a document, they could help their dead loved ones leave purgatory sooner, rather than later. The theory was that Christ and the saints had earned so many "bonus points" with God through all their good works that this provided a huge "treasury of merits" the Church could tap into and dole out to penitent sinners. Luther realized that this whole system and theory was entirely contrary to the Word of God and posted a set of Ninety-Five Theses challenging his fellow academics to a debate about it. This event set in motion the chain of events that today we know as the Lutheran Reformation.

Christ's life of perfect obedience to God's Law with His perfect, innocent suffering and death would provide the full and complete payment for sin. Psalm 49:7 states, "No man can ransom another, or give to God the price of his life." Jesus tells us in Mark 10:45, "The Son of Man came not to be served but to serve, and to give His life as a ransom for many."

And note particularly what Paul writes in Romans 3:22–24: "For there is no distinction: for all have sinned and fall short of the glory of God, and are justified by His grace as a gift, through the redemption that is in Christ Jesus." There is absolutely no difference between any mere man. All human beings have sinned and fallen short of the glory of God. *All* means all. Had Christ been merely a man, He, too, would have been part of the "all" of humanity. Only the God-man was spared the fate all humans share in common.

In Galatians 3:13, Paul elaborates further on the fact that "Christ redeemed us from the curse of the law by becoming a curse for us." What does this mean? It means simply that the Law of God, which is good and holy, becomes for those who break it a curse, for we fall far, far short of God's perfect standards. We are therefore cursed and condemned to eternal death and hell. Separated from a holy God, unholy people have only one fate. But Christ Jesus steps in and pays the required ransom of holiness: His own perfect life and innocent suffering and death. That shedding of His blood is what cleanses us from all sin. It was part of God's plan. Paul writes in Galatians 4:4–5, "When the fullness of time had come, God sent His Son, born of woman, born under the law, to redeem those who were under the law, so that we might receive adoption as sons."

Only God's Blood Would Work

The blood of a mere man would never suffice to serve as the atoning sacrifice and ransom for sin. We turn to Peter's First Letter, where we read, "Knowing that you were ransomed from the futile ways inherited from your forefathers, not with perishable things such as silver or gold, but with the precious blood of Christ, like that of a lamb without blemish or spot" (1 Peter 1:18–19). Here Peter has in view the great prophetic chapter of Isaiah 53, where the prophet states, "He was oppressed, and He was afflicted, yet He opened not His mouth; like a lamb that is led to the slaughter, and like a sheep that before its shearers is silent, so He opened not His mouth" (v. 7), and "He was pierced for our transgressions; He was crushed for our iniquities; upon Him was the chastisement that brought us peace, and with His wounds we are healed" (v. 5).

And finally, Christ had to be true God in order that He might overcome our ancient enemies: death and the devil. Paul writes, "Thanks be to God, who gives us the victory through our Lord Jesus Christ" (1 Corinthians 15:57). In 2 Timothy 1:10, we read, "Our Savior Christ Jesus [has] abolished death," and in Hebrews 2:14, "Since therefore the children share in flesh and blood, He Himself likewise partook of the same things, that though death He might destroy the one who has the power of death, that is, the devil."

Therefore, we rejoice to bear witness and give joyful public confession to the fact that Jesus Christ is the God-man who in loving service lived perfectly in our place and poured out His lifeblood as the sacrifice for the sins of the world. This reality shapes our entire lives, as Paul explains, "You were bought with a price. So glorify God in your body" (1 Corinthians 6:20).

MAKING CONNECTIONS

One of the more powerful images you will see in many churches and in traditional Christian art and architecture is a lamb. The symbol is referred to with the ancient Latin words **Agnus Dei**, which means "lamb of God." It is based on what John the Baptist said when he saw Jesus coming toward him: "Behold, the Lamb of God, who takes away the sin of the world!" (John 1:29).

False Teachings about Christ in Church History

(Or "There Is Nothing New Under the Sun")

It is important that we understand the history of the Early Church so we can have a better appreciation for what, precisely, our fathers and mothers in the faith struggled with and through for our sake. We have a rich tradition and heritage of truth passed down from generation to generation of Christians. There never has been a "golden age" for the Church. That is simply the stuff of legend and fantasy. People who try to recapture this mythical golden age are doomed to failure. Every movement to try to "return to the greatest days of Christianity" results in nothing more than yet another cult or sect teaching false doctrines. And so it has ever been.

Was the Lutheran Reformation an attempt to restore the past? No. It has always been about reforming and renewing the Church with the Gospel, because it has always been all about Jesus. It is very important that Christians today understand the Church's historic debates about the person and work of Jesus Christ so we do not stumble back into errors that were identified centuries ago and determined to be contrary to Holy Scripture.

It is a witness to the astounding impact Christ made on all who saw and heard Him that there arose various arguments over whether or not He was truly a man and whether or not, or to what extent, He was true God. There was something amazing about this man. The Gospel writers and the other writers of the New Testament books were used by the Holy Spirit to provide as much information about Christ as we need to come to trust in Him as our Savior. They do not necessarily provide all the answers to every question we may have, and here is where problems arise. Speculations not based on God's Word lead to a whole host of misunderstandings and false teachings about Christ.

Adoptionism. Early on there were speculations floating around among groups like the Gnostics who emphasized obtaining secret or hidden knowledge about God. The word *Gnostic* comes from the Greek word for knowledge. As part of their speculations, there arose views that would later be called "adoptionism" when referring to Christ. The heresy of adoptionism arose in the second century and denied the pre-existence of the divine nature of Christ. Rather, it said that the man Jesus of Nazareth was "adopted" by God for the mission on which God sent Him. They believed God tested Jesus in various ways (at His fasting, etc.), and as result of passing the tests given by God, He was adopted as a son by God at His Baptism and rewarded for all He did. A key leader in the Adoptionist heresy was Theodotus of Byzantium. Victor, Bishop of Rome from AD 190–198, issued the definitive refutation and rejection of this heresy.

Docetism was a movement deriving its name from the Greek word *dokeo*, which means "to seem." In this heresy, it was taught that Jesus only appeared to have a human body, but was in fact not actually human, was not the incarnate Son of God, but simply the Son of God appearing to have taken on a human form. It's a testimony to the impression Jesus' miracles made on people that a heresy arose questioning how it could be possible for Jesus to be true man, while it was agreed by all He was truly God. This heresy was attributed to the Gnostic sects, and we see much of these speculations about Jesus in the so-called "Gospel of Peter," which was an account of Christ's life written by the Gnostics. Significant Early Church theologians, such as Ignatius of Antioch, Irenaeus, and Hippolytus thoroughly refuted Docetism, and it died out. Still, it was formally condemned, along with many other historic heresies at the Council of Carthage in AD 451.

Apolinarianism is a heresy named after the man named Apollinaris the Younger, who was actually a Christian bishop in Laodicea—which is in modern-day Syria—around AD 360. Here again this heresy also denied the true and complete humanity of Jesus, teaching that Christ did not have an actual human mind, but was instead completely divine, with the human nature simply along for the ride, so to speak. The heresy was formally renounced at the Council of Constantinople in AD 381.

Arianism was the most significant heresy concerning Christ in the Early Church. Arianism spread like wildfire throughout the known Church of the time during the second century and into the third. The man, Arius of Alexandria, Egypt, lived roughly from AD 250–336. He spread the teaching that Jesus was simply a "creature" who was "begotten" of the Father, but there was a time when He did not exist. In this view, only the Father may properly said to be God, but Jesus is the one who represents the pure and holy Father in time, a creation of God, who then in turn was adopted by the Father and appointed to be His Son. Jesus is not to be worshiped as God, but simply because of His preeminent role as first in God's creation. Arius popularized a phrase, "There was a time when He was not." It was spread through hymns and other public teachings and teachers. The Council of Nicaea in AD 325 thoroughly refuted the Arian heresy. The orthodox Christian pastor Athanasius devoted most of his life working hard to expose and refute the heresy, and his great writing, *On the Incarnation of the Word of God*, remains a classic and timeless explanation of how Jesus Christ is truly God of God, Light of Light, very God of very God. The saying arose, "What He [Christ] did not assume, He did not redeem." In other words, if Jesus was not actually the Son of God taking on a real human nature, then we can never know and be certain that we have been redeemed and saved by God taking on this human nature.

Nestorianism arose from the speculations of Nestorius of Antioch, Bishop of Constantinople in AD 428. Nestorius taught that Mary gave birth only to the human nature of Jesus, not to the Son of God. Nestorius did not want Mary to be referred to as the mother of God, which of course, she is. The heresy essentially resulted in a division of the human and divine nature of Christ, suggesting that He consisted of two persons, not one person. And so, if the heresy is true, there is never any true communication of attributes between the divine and human nature and therefore robs us of the comfort of knowing that the Son of God did take on human flesh and as one person, with two natures, redeemed us. Nestorianism was formally rejected at the Council of Ephesus in AD 431.

Monophysitism, also known as Eutychianism after the leader, Eutyches of Constantinople (AD 380–456) was an overreaction to the Nestorian heresy and taught that the humanity of Jesus was absorbed entirely into the divine nature, mixed entirely with it to the point we are unable to speak of two natures in Christ, but only one nature, the divine nature. The Greek word for "nature" is *physis* and *mono* means "one." The monophysite heresy teaches that Jesus only has one nature, a nature that is something new and different than either the divine or human nature in Christ. This third unique nature is a blending or mixing of the divine and human natures. This heresy is still held to by Coptic Christians and a few other smaller groups like them.

The Fourth Ecumenical Council of Chalcedon clarified and corrected this heresy in AD 451 and at that same time again rejected Nestorianism. It established a set formula for properly articulating the doctrine of the two natures in Christ and describes them thus: "We teach . . . one and the same Christ, Son, Lord, Only-begotten, known in two natures, without confusion, without change, without division, without separation." The first two phrases, "without confusion, without change," refute the heresy of Nestorius and the second two phrases, "without division and without separation," refute the heresy of Eutyches. While this may all sound hopefully complex, there is a profound impact on how we understand the salvation Christ has worked for us.

Monothelitism arose in the years following the Council of Chalcedon and was intended to provide a refutation of the monophysite heresy, but as so often happens, in trying to offer a correction, it went too far. The name for this heresy derives from the Greek words *mono*, or "alone," and *thelos*, or "will." This heresy taught that Jesus definitely does have two natures but only a single will. Instead of having two cooperating wills, the will of the divine nature of the Son of God, and the will of the human nature, there is only one operative will in Christ, said to be a divine *"energia"* or *"energy"* that animated Him. Sergius of Constantinople from AD 610–638 was responsible for propagating this teaching, and his views were formally condemned by the Third Council of Constantinople, the Sixth of the so-called Seven Ecumenical Councils, in AD 681.

We can find elements and mixtures of all these ancient Christological heresies, as they are referred to, in various modern era teachings and movements. For example, the Jehovah's Witnesses are de facto Arians in how they regard Jesus, going so far as to change the wording of John's Gospel: "In the beginning was the Word, . . . and the Word was God" (1:1) to "the Word was a God." It is a glaring example of how heresy takes root. Many Christian cults contain elements of ancient heresies. The non-Christian religion of Mormonism contains elements of a whole host of ancient religious errors and Christian heresies that touch on not simply Christ but on the Holy Trinity and other areas.

Jesus predicted during His life that false teachers would arise after His departure: "Many will come in My name, saying, 'I am the Christ,' and they will lead many astray" (Matthew 24:5). The human desire to delve into matters that finally are beyond our understanding is a dangerous temptation. Each of the heresies we have mentioned put the Gospel itself at risk when it questioned or denied the true person and work of Jesus Christ.

The price of faithfulness and orthodoxy is eternal vigilance. That's why those who serve in confessional Lutheran congregations as pastors and teachers are pledged to the Book of Concord, which contains the Lutheran Confessions. In the Book of Concord, all these ancient heresies are named and explicitly condemned and rejected. No faithful Lutheran pastor should ever be, in any way, teaching any of these heresies.

Study Questions

1. Why is it absolutely necessary that Jesus is both true God *and* true man?

2. Lambs are infamously known to be helpless creatures. But Jesus is often called the "Lamb of God." Why is this an appropriate name for the all-knowing, all-powerful Savior of the world?

3. Read 1 Corinthians 6:19–20 and dwell on the word *price*. What is Paul making sure you understand? What does it mean to "glorify God in your body"?

4. The Bible doesn't necessarily offer answers to every question you have. Why is that okay? What happens when you make speculations that aren't necessarily based on God's Word?

Visit lutheranism101.com to download the free Leader Guide.

5. What was the most significant heresy in the Early Church concerning Christ? What did those who held this view believe? Why is it false? (p. 85)

Discussion Questions

1. In the Middle Ages, Luther disagreed with many teachings of the Roman Church, and so he posted his Ninety-Five Theses on the front doors of the local church—a common practice in Luther's time to start a discussion. Today, how can you respectfully disagree with teachings contrary to Scripture? What forums are available to you that are most conducive to healthy debate and discourse? Then, consider this: how prepared are you to defend your beliefs?

2. Think about the temptations Jesus faced during His life on earth. He went without food for several weeks when He easily could have turned a stone into bread. He was beaten, spat on, and crucified. He could have rejected those men, refused to love them. But He didn't. Rather, He asked His father to forgive them. Jesus displayed perfect obedience. Think about your greatest temptations. How quickly do you succumb to them? On the other hand, how do you resist the devil's schemes and temptations?

3. Read Matthew 24:5. What warning does Jesus give to His disciples? How is this warning relevant to Christians today?

Visit lutheranism101.com to download the free Leader Guide.

4. Why is it important for you to understand the foundational teachings of Scripture instead of leaving such discussions and study to the theologians?

PART THREE

What you'll learn about:

- Jesus did not always use His Son of God powers.
- As true man, Jesus humbled Himself in order to accomplish His work of being our Savior.
- God wore diapers.

What Jesus Does for You, Then and Now

Now it is time to move even more deeply into the precise "how and why" of what Jesus did for you during His earthly life and ministry. Then we will examine how what He did then is applied to you today. We'll cover the two distinct phases of Christ's life on earth: the states of humiliation and exaltation. As we cover these topics you will understand the depth and enormity of His agony and bitter death for you as He suffered one of the most horrible forms of capital punishment ever used: crucifixion.

CHAPTER 7

The State of Humiliation

In This Chapter

- While Jesus had awesome God powers, He didn't always use them.
- Jesus was born of a virgin. It's a fact.
- Jesus lived a servant life to teach us about serving others.

Christ's state of humiliation refers to the fact that He did not always use, or did not fully use at all times, the powers He had as the Son of God. We can also look on this as Christ concealing at times the fact that He was truly God. As we discuss this, though, we must avoid the error of thinking or suggesting that Christ ever gave up His divine nature or ever was without it. Setting it aside in the sense of not fully using His divine powers does not mean He was ever without the divine nature. Paul explains it this way in Philippians 2:5–8:

> Have this mind among yourselves, which is yours in Christ Jesus, who, though he was in the form of God, did not count equality with God a thing to be grasped, but emptied himself, by taking the form of a servant, being born in the likeness of men. And being found in human form, he humbled himself by becoming obedient to the point of death, even death on a cross.

Here Paul beautifully summarizes the reality of Christ's state of humiliation. The word *form* can also be translated "nature." In order to save us, Christ willingly did not use all the attributes of His divinity at all times, but took on the form of a servant—His human form—being born like we are born, living as we live, dying as we die, to offer Himself up as the full and final sacrifice for all sins.

NEED TO KNOW

Humiliation: Christ humbled Himself by not exercising fully, according to His human nature, the rights and powers that rightfully belonged to Him as the Son of God. Christ humbled Himself according to His human nature. The divine nature was not capable of being humbled or exalted or changed in state or condition in any way.

So, let's look at Christ's walk "down the ladder" of His humiliation as we have it in the Apostles' Creed:

Ladder of Christ's Humiliation

Conceived by the Holy Spirit,
> born of the Virgin Mary,
>> suffered under Pontius Pilate,
>>> was crucified,
>>>> died
>>>>> and was buried.

Born of a Virgin?

"Oh, really?" If we are honest about it, that is probably how many of us reacted when we first heard the Christian Church's teaching that Christ was conceived without the normal human act of procreation. Imagine how Joseph, Mary's fiancée felt, when he first heard about it. The virgin birth was certainly even more of a scandalous event in the time of Jesus than a child born out of wedlock is today. Sadly, it has become fairly common for couples to conceive children before they are married, but in Jesus' time such behavior resulted in an incredible amount of shame, embarrassment, and scandal. In fact, fornication was punishable even by death in some circumstances.

Sometimes we hear expectant husbands and wives refer to a "miraculous birth" after a long period of hoping and waiting for a pregnancy, but there was only one actual and genuine "miraculous birth," the birth of Jesus of Nazareth. Without the involvement of any human male, Mary conceived a child in her womb by the power of the Holy Spirit. It is a teaching that has been ridiculed and laughed at since the earliest days of the Church, but it remains a bedrock reality of the Christian faith.

Scripture teaches that in the virginal conception of Jesus, the Son of God, He was given a true human body and soul in the womb of the Virgin Mary. Luke 1:35 explains what happened this way: "The Holy Spirit will come upon you, and the power of the Most High will overshadow you; therefore the child to be born will be called holy—the Son of God." Joseph, who had recently become engaged to be married to Mary, was extremely baffled by Mary's report that an angel had visited her to announce that she was to be the mother of a son. God stepped in, though, to reveal to Joseph that he should not be troubled at this. "Joseph, son of David, do not fear to take Mary as your wife, for that which is conceived in her is from the

FROM THE BIBLE

Faith is the assurance of things hoped for, the conviction of things not seen. (Hebrews 11:1)

NEED TO KNOW

incarnation: The word *incarnation* comes from two Latin words, *in* and *carne* (which means "flesh"). Literally, then, it means "in the flesh."

FROM THE BIBLE

Great indeed, we confess, is the mystery of godliness: He was manifested in the flesh, vindicated by the Spirit, seen by angels, proclaimed among the nations, believed on in the world, taken up in glory. (1 Timothy 3:16)

Holy Spirit" (Matthew 1:20). Most of us are aware of the ordinary stresses and tensions that arise with any upcoming wedding, but can you imagine how Joseph must have felt? Mary had humbly accepted the angel's message to her and "treasured up all these things, pondering them in her heart" (Luke 2:19). We are called to do the same. Because we cannot fully comprehend or understand how these things are so, we accept that they are so, by God's gracious revelation to us through Holy Scripture.

We should be careful to speak very specifically at this point about the conception, not the birth of Christ—though, of course, most people referring to the birth of Jesus have in mind also His conception. But it is important to separate the conception of Jesus from His birth. The circumstances of His birth are one thing. The fact of His conception in the womb of a woman who had never had sexual intercourse with a man is quite another.

The Great Danger of "Modern" Christianity

Modern liberal Christianity has discarded much of the historic confessions and truths of biblical Christianity. Liberal Christianity denies the incarnation and the entire doctrine of the two natures in Christ, so it is no surprise that Christ's virginal conception is viewed as little more than an ancient fairy tale. What liberal Christianity considers to be simply unthinkable, Paul simply says is a great mystery of the faith (1 Timothy 3:16). Liberal Christianity has embraced a rationalist and naturalist view of all things. Whatever is in conflict with such assumptions is deemed impossible, myth, or mere fantasy.

Martin Luther beautifully explains the meaning of the virgin conception and birth of Christ:

Therefore the Seed of the Woman could not be an ordinary man; for He had to crush the power of the devil, sin, and death; and since all men are subject to the devil on account of sin and death, He most assuredly had to be without sin. Now, human nature does not bear such seed or fruit . . . for they are all under the devil because of their sin. . . . So the only means to accomplish the desired end was this: the Seed must be a truly natural Son of the woman, not born, however, of the woman in a natural way, but by an extraordinary act of God, in order that the Scriptures might be fulfilled that He should be the Seed of only a woman, not of a man; for the text [Gen. 3:15] clearly says that He shall be the Seed of a woman. (St. L., XX, 1796 f.)[1]

BELIEVE, TEACH, CONFESS

Mary, the most blessed Virgin, did not bear a mere man. But, as the angel <Gabriel> testifies, she bore a man who is truly the Son of the most high God [Luke 1:35]. He showed His divine majesty even in His mother's womb, because He was born of a virgin, without violating her virginity. Therefore, she is truly the mother of God and yet has remained a virgin. (FC SD VIII 24)

We need to be clear on this point. The incarnation itself was in no way a humiliation of God, but a gracious condescension on His part. The humble circumstances in which it all took place are what make it part of the humiliation of the Son of God.

The birth of the Son of God in such a meek and lowly way is also part of His humiliation. Imagine if you or I had been planning on how best to send the Son of God into the world. I'm sure all of us would have come up with something quite a bit grander and more impressive than how it actually happened. Instead, "She gave birth to her firstborn son and wrapped Him in swaddling cloths and laid Him in a manger, because there was no place for them in the inn" (Luke 2:7).

No Compromise Is Possible Concerning the Virgin Birth

We must never allow any compromise on the fact of the virginal conception and birth of Christ. Consider the alternative if it is not true. It would mean simply that the Virgin Mary was a deceitful young woman who had engaged in promiscuous sex outside of marriage and had managed to rope into her scheme the man Joseph, and together the two of them perpetuated a fraud and kept up the lie as sinful con artists. The entire life and ministry of Christ Himself would be based on a lie and

---

1   John Theodore Mueller, *Christian Dogmatics*, electronic ed. (St. Louis: Concordia, 1999), 293.

MAKING CONNECTIONS

The whole truth and nothing but the truth, so help me God! This is the attitude we must take when we approach the Scriptures. We must not treat the Bible like a buffet line, where we pick and choose the parts we like and pass by the rest. No, all Scripture is inspired by God and is suitable for use in the Church and by every Christian. (See 2 Timothy 3:16.)

NEED TO KNOW

Isaiah's prophecies of Christ culminate in the four Suffering Servant songs (Isaiah 42:1–9; 49:1–13; 50:4–11; 52:13–53:12). The center of the final poem (53:1–9) details the Servant's rejection and suffering as the Lamb who is sacrificed for our sins. Yet the poem begins (52:10–12) and concludes (53:10–12) with His victorious exaltation.

would remain only the stuff of legend and myth. So when people ask, "Do I have to believe in the virgin birth to be a Christian?" The answer simply is, "Yes. Anyone who claims to be a Christian would never deny it."

A Life of Humble Service and Sacrifice

During His life, suffering, and death, Christ endured great humiliation. We know He endured poverty. He was held in contempt by neighbors, by supposed friends, and even by His own family members at times. He was persecuted for what He preached and what He did. Even as an infant, He was persecuted. Herod, the Jewish king in Palestine at the time of Jesus' birth, went out of his way to try to murder Jesus when he heard of His birth from the Wise Men (see Matthew 2:13). Consider, for example, what Paul writes in 2 Corinthians 8:9: "Though He was rich, yet for your sake He became poor, so that you by His poverty might become rich." The One through whom all things were made came into this world of ours, giving it all up, assuming the poverty of our sinful condition upon Himself so we might be given all the riches of God's grace and mercy. In Matthew 8:20, Jesus says, "Foxes have holes, and birds of the air have nests, but the Son of Man has nowhere to lay His head." Isaiah the prophet had long ago said of the Christ, "He was despised and rejected by men, a man of sorrows and acquainted with grief; and as one from whom men hide their faces, He was despised, and we esteemed Him not" (53:3). The message of Jesus so outraged and offended the religious leaders of His day that Jesus said, "You seek to kill Me, a man who has told you the truth that I heard from God" (John 8:40).

A number of people from Jesus' hometown even attempted to throw Him off a cliff after He rebuked them for unbelief. "When they heard these things, all in the synagogue were filled with wrath. And they rose up and drove Him out of the town and brought Him to the brow of the hill on which their town was built, so that they could throw Him down the cliff. But passing through their midst, He went away" (Luke 4:28–30). And later in the temple, the crowds started to pick up stones to stone Him, "but Jesus hid Himself and went out of the temple" (John 8:59).

Understanding the Enormity of His Suffering and Death

And we need look no further than the great suffering and agony Jesus underwent in both body and soul as He laid down His life for us. His physical torture and extreme agony on the cross are the ultimate humiliation of the Son of God. During His trial, torture, and execution by crucifixion, our Lord Jesus Christ underwent extreme agony both in His body and His soul. Under the Roman governor, Pontius Pilate, He was killed in the most shameful and brutal manner of execution known in the Roman Empire: crucifixion.

Before being nailed to the cross, He was "scourged," a form of whipping involving a Roman instrument of punishment designed to inflict the maximum amount of pain and damage

MAKING CONNECTIONS

Stricken, smitten, and afflicted,
See Him dying on the tree!
'Tis the Christ, by man rejected;
Yes, my soul, 'tis He, 'tis He!
'Tis the long-expected Prophet,
David's Son, yet David's Lord;
Proofs I see sufficient of it:
'Tis the true and faithful Word.
Tell me, ye who hear Him groaning,
Was there ever grief like His?
Friends through fear His cause disowning,
Foes insulting His distress;
Many hands were raised to wound Him,
None would intervene to save;
But the deepest stroke that pierced Him
Was the stroke that justice gave.
Ye who think of sin but lightly
Nor suppose the evil great
Here may view its nature rightly,
Here its guilt may estimate.
Mark the sacrifice appointed,
See who bears the awful load;
'Tis the Word, the Lord's anointed,
Son of Man and Son of God.
Here we have a firm foundation,
Here the refuge of the lost:
Christ, the Rock of our salvation,
Is the name of which we boast;
Lamb of God, for sinners wounded,
Sacrifice to cancel guilt!
None shall ever be confounded
Who on Him their hope have built.
  (*LSB* 451)

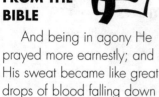

to a human being. All the while He was mocked and made fun of by His tormenters.

We read in John 19:1–3:

> Pilate took Jesus and flogged Him. And the soldiers twisted together a crown of thorns and put it on His head and arrayed Him in a purple robe. They came up to Him, saying, "Hail, King of the Jews!" and struck Him with their hands."

The four Gospels each record various aspects of Christ's crucifixion. We know that on the cross He died in horrendous pain and agony. While on the cross, "Jesus cried out with a loud voice, . . . 'My God, My God, why have You forsaken Me?' " (Matthew 27:46). What does this mean, that Christ was "forsaken" by God? First, He was never actually "forsaken by God," but in the midst of His horrible death, the human nature of Christ felt utterly abandoned and forsaken. His Father permitted Him to go through this in order to pay the ultimate penalty for all our sins. The Father permitted His incarnate Son, according to His human nature, to bear every sin of every human being, past, present, and future. In that suffering, Jesus felt completely and utterly alone and forsaken. And at last we read in John 19:30, "He bowed His head and gave up His spirit." It is important to note that Jesus gave up His spirit. He willingly laid down His life. It was not taken from Him by sinful men. No, they merely were the instruments of His execution. The Son of God knew full well what was happening and why, and He therefore willingly, and in the greatest act of loving kindness toward sinful humanity, laid down His life for us.

And then, one more act of humiliation: His burial. As in life, so also in death, Jesus had no permanent home, nowhere to lay His head (Luke 9:58). He had no tomb of His own. There was no family plot waiting to receiving Him, and so He was buried in a borrowed tomb and remained there for three days. While in the tomb, His body suffered no decay (Acts 13:37). A more complete narrative of His burial is found in Mark 15:42–47.

The Challenge of the Virgin Birth

by Rev. Klemet I. Preus

Of all the miracles in the New Testament, it strikes me that the story of the virgin birth of Jesus is the most difficult to verify or to falsify, making it an easy target for skeptics.

Most miracles are done before crowds, providing all sorts of witnesses. But the angel appeared to Mary while she was alone. Further, immediately after the report of a miracle you can disprove or prove it. But this is extremely difficult with the virgin birth. We may actually be able to explain some of those miraculous events.

Now I speak as an unbelieving skeptic, Lloyd, but I trust that God will forgive me if I can convince you. Let's say that the Bible is false, and that you shouldn't necessarily believe it just because it says so. What if we can come up with an alternate theory of the birth of Jesus? Let's hypothesize that Joseph and Mary had an affair and didn't want to expose themselves to the public humiliation of a pregnancy in the small town of Nazareth. Joseph, aware of the census that had been ordered by Caesar Augustus, had a hasty wedding and decided to travel to Bethlehem for his child's birth. An innkeeper, seeing the young family camped out in the town square, had compassion on the family and offered them a place to stay. Eventually, Joseph fled to Egypt and returned to Bethlehem a couple of years later with toddler and wife in tow. No one would be the wiser regarding the timing of the little boy's birth relative to the wedding. Perhaps Mary made up the story of the angel announcing the birth of Jesus. Let's say that when Jesus became famous, she embellished the events of His birth to give His popularity a boost.

Now that's an alternate theory which does, I believe, take into consideration most or all of the data from the Bible. It is certainly more plausible to our human understanding, especially if you don't believe in miracles. But there are a couple of problems with this alternate story. First, there is no evidence from any eyewitness or anyone close to the story that my version is actually what happened. We can theorize two thousand years later that this story makes more sense, but that doesn't make it true. In fact, if we were honest, we would have to admit that the only reason anyone would believe this alternate explanation of the facts is to explain away the story of the miracle. People just don't want to believe in the virgin birth. There is, frankly, an anti-miracle bias that forces people to accept alternate explanations.

There is a second, more formidable flaw with the theory that Joseph is the biological father of the child. Was Jesus really so popular as to necessitate His mother making up a story about His birth? Actually, Jesus' popularity had seriously waned in the days leading up to His death. In John 6 it is reported that most of His disciples had left Him. And don't forget that when He was crucified, it is reported that all His disciples ran away—one was even naked. He was certainly not popular while hanging on the cross. Matthew wrote his Gospel around AD 50, and Luke in about AD 55–60. These two obviously believed that Jesus was born of a virgin. What happened between the year AD 30 and the year AD 55 to make them believe this of Jesus? How did a crucified prophet get so popular that His disciples would believe such an amazing claim? It would require an event more profoundly miraculous and inexplicable by natural standards than the virgin birth itself. It would require the resurrection of Jesus from the grave.

—From *What They Need to Hear* (St. Louis: Concordia, 2013), 27–28

Study Questions

1. What are the six ladder-like components of Christ's humiliation?

2. When thinking about Christ's humiliation, why is it important to separate His conception from His birth?

3. John 19:1 says, "Pilate took Jesus and flogged Him." Why did Pilate do this, if, earlier, he said, "I find no guilt in Him" (18:38)?

4. Read Matthew 27:46. Did God truly forsake Jesus? Why or why not? Does God ever forsake you? Explain.

5. What is the significance of John 19:30, "He bowed His head and gave up His spirit"?

Visit lutheranism101.com to download the free Leader Guide.

Discussion Questions

1. What kind of relationship do you think Mary and Jesus had? Read John 19:25–27. What do Jesus' actions say about His feelings toward His mother?

2. Liberal Christianity has embraced a rationalistic and naturalist view of all things, deeming anything in conflict with such views to be impossible, myth, or mere fantasy. What is the danger in adopting these liberal points of view?

3. Read John 19:1–3. God permitted His Son, according to His human nature, to take on the punishment of every sin of every human being, including you. Read John 19:1–3 again; this time, put yourself among those who crucified Jesus: "*I* took Jesus and flogged Him. And *I* twisted together a crown of thorns and put it on His head and arrayed Him in a purple robe. *I* went up to Him, saying, 'Hail, king of the Jews!' and struck Him with *my* hands." How does rereading the verse in this way impact your understanding of God's immense love for you?

CHAPTER 8

Christ's Work of Redemption and Atonement

In This Chapter

- You are the reason God the Son humbled Himself and became man.
- See how the "then and there" is applied to the "here and now."
- A closer look at crucifixion shows us the depth of God's love.

TECHNICAL STUFF

atonement. From an old French term for being "at one." Reconciliation between parties that were previously divided. One man's life given as a sacrifice and ransom to redeem all others.

Scripture reveals that in every way, at every point, during His humiliation, Christ was doing everything for us and for our salvation. Let's take a closer look at the heart of the Christian faith: the doctrine of the atonement.

To Redeem Me

Why did Christ put Himself through all the various aspects of His humiliation? Why did He go through a life of abnegation, degradation, and the most horrible, bitter, painful suffering and death that one can hardly imagine? Why? For us! Christ voluntarily went through all that He did, humbling Himself precisely so that He could redeem you and me, lost and condemned creatures as we are. Let's review some key texts from Scripture.

In Isaiah 53:4–5, we read, "Surely He has borne our griefs and carried our sorrows; yet we esteemed Him stricken, smitten by God, and afflicted. But He was pierced for our transgressions; He was crushed for our iniquities; upon Him was the chastisement that brought us peace, and with His wounds we are healed."

This passage is one of the most crystal clear explanations of the purpose of Christ's life, suffering, and death that we have in the Scriptures. It all boils down to two words: for you. Everything Christ has done, He has done it for you. "This is My body, given for you. This is My blood, shed for you." God made His Son, who was absolutely sinless, to become sin for us. We, who are born into this world as children of Adam and Eve, inherit at the moment of our conception the curse of original sin and all the death and sin and evil consequences that came into this world because of our first parent's sin. We see this all around us in the world. We see it in our own lives and in our very bodies. We cannot escape the consequences of sin in this world, but Christ rescues us through His perfect death on our behalf, which the heavenly Father accepts as the payment for our sin.

BELIEVE, TEACH, CONFESS

Sin originated from one man, Adam. By his disobedience, all people were made sinners and became subject to death and the devil. This is called original or the chief sin. . . . This hereditary sin is such a deep corruption of nature that no reason can understand it. Rather, it must be believed from the revelation of Scripture. (See Psalm 51:5; Romans 6:12–13; Exodus 33:3; Genesis 3:7–19.) (SA III II 1, 3)

Behold, the Lamb of God!

Christ has redeemed us from all sins, from death, and from the power of the devil. When John the Baptist recognized the Savior, he cried out, "Behold, the Lamb of God, who takes away the sin of the world!" (John 1:29). The concept of the sacrificial lamb was integral to the self-identify of God's people from the time that the Hebrew people were slaves in Egypt long before the birth of Christ. They were unable to free themselves. They were doomed to lives of misery under the harsh rule of the Egyptians. They were effectively "lost" as a people due to circumstances entirely out of their control. But God stepped in and rescued them from the bondage of slavery. After nine horrific plagues, the last and final plague inflicted on the people of Egypt was the death of all firstborn males. To save the lives of firstborn Hebrew males, God ordered His people to kill a lamb and brush the blood of that lamb on their doorways. Seeing the blood, the angel of death would pass over that house, thereby allowing the child to live. This was the first Passover (Exodus 12).

Throughout the history of the Jewish people, this annual remembrance of the great passing over of death and the rescue by God was observed in every Jewish home and still is. But with the coming of Jesus, we have the ultimate Lamb of God,

MAKING CONNECTIONS

In worship, directly before receiving the body and blood of Christ, we sing the canticle, called "Agnus Dei." This is Latin for "Lamb of God." We sing this as a prayer to the now-present Christ under the elements of Holy Communion, asking Him to give us that peace that passes all understanding:

Lamb of God, You take away the sin of the world; have mercy on us.

Lamb of God, You take away the sin of the world; have mercy on us.

Lamb of God, You take away the sin of the world; grant us peace.

TECHNICAL STUFF

confession. The act by which one admits or confesses sin(s) and the guilt of sin.

whose blood covered the crossbeams of the cross for us! He died, an innocent sacrifice, so God would redeem us from our sins and from the curse of death and the power of the devil. The writer of the Letter to the Hebrews explains it beautifully this way:

> Since therefore the children share in flesh and blood, he himself likewise partook of the same things, that through death he might destroy the one who has the power of death, that is, the devil, and deliver all those who through fear of death were subject to lifelong slavery. . . .Therefore, He had to be made like His brothers in every respect, so that He might become a merciful and faithful high priest in service of God, to make propitiation for the sins of the people. (Hebrews 2:14–15, 17)

A Real Savior for Real Sinners: Like You and Me

Christ took upon Himself your guilt and the punishment you deserved. He took on the guilt and punishment of the entire world. Romans 5:19 says, "So by the one man's obedience the many will be made righteous," and in 2 Corinthians 5:21, we read, "He made Him to be sin who knew no sin, so that in Him we might become the righteousness of God." Finally, in Galatians 3:13, Paul says, "Christ redeemed us from the curse of the law by becoming a curse for us—for it is written, 'Cursed is everyone who is hanged on a tree.'"

He removes our guilt, takes our punishment, and frees us from the slavery of sin. Jesus says in John 8:34, 36, "Truly, truly I say to you, everyone who practices sin is a slave to sin. . . . So if the

Son sets you free, you will be free indeed." And in 1 Peter 2:24, we read, "He Himself bore our sins in His body on the tree, that we might die to sin and live to righteousness. By His wounds you have been healed." Here Peter clearly is hearkening back to Isaiah 53. Jesus lived, suffered, and died so that each and every one of our sins would be forgiven.

You know what your sins are. You know them precisely. There are likely many things about yourself and your sins that you would never want anyone to know, and, at times, you have probably, like everyone else, taken elaborate steps to forget, ignore, overlook, excuse, or justify your sins to yourself. But God knows. As the psalmist wrote, "For I know my transgressions, and my sin is ever before me" (51:3). For each and every one of your sins, Jesus offered Himself as the perfect atoning sacrifice, which God accepted as payment for all those sins.

Jesus rescues us not only from sin but also from death, which is sin's ultimate penalty in this life. He rescues us from the eternal penalty of eternal death, an unending separation from God in the never-ending fire of hell. Through all that He suffered, through His death, and because of His glorious resurrection, Christ has triumphed over our great enemy: death. Now He gives each of us eternal life. We need not fear death. Death does not have the final word in your life. Jesus does.

Paul joyfully exclaims in light of the resurrection, "'O death, where is your victory? O death, where is your sting?' The sting of death is sin, and the power of sin is the law. But thanks be to God, who gives us the victory through our Lord Jesus Christ" (1 Corinthians 15:55–57). Jesus Christ has "brought life and immortality to light through the gospel" (2 Timothy 1:10). In Christ, "according to His great mercy, He has caused us to be born again to a living hope through the resurrection of Jesus Christ from the dead" (1 Peter 1:3). Can there possibly be better news than this? No! This is precisely why the message of Jesus is "Gospel," which means "a proclamation of good news."

MAKING CONNECTIONS

In the Lutheran service of Holy Communion, the service begins with a confession of sins, like this one: "I, a poor, miserable sinner, confess unto You all my sins and iniquities with which I have ever offended You and justly deserved Your temporal and eternal punishment. But I am heartily sorry for them and sincerely repent of them, and I pray You of Your boundless mercy and for the sake of the holy, innocent, bitter sufferings and death of Your beloved Son, Jesus Christ, to be gracious and merciful to me, a poor, sinful being" (*LSB*, p. 184).

MAKING CONNECTIONS

"Have you been born again? Are you a born-again Christian?" We hear these questions from people in denominations that, ironically, do not believe in the power of Holy Baptism. All who have been baptized into Christ can say with full assurance, "Yes, I've been born again!" And to the question, "Are you a born-again Christian?" We can say simply, "Is there any other kind?" Many non-denominational and other "decision theology" church bodies claim that being "born again" is a deliberate act of will and a decision that person "makes for Jesus." But nothing could be further from the truth. It is God who works faith in our hearts, and in and through Holy Baptism we have the promise given to us that we have been forgiven through the work of Jesus Christ. "He has caused us to be born again," says Peter (1 Peter 1:3). Yes, you are a born-again Christian. There is no other kind.

Be On Guard!

But wait, there's more! Though we are free from sin, free from death, and rescued from the power of the devil, that old tempter still prowls around like a roaring lion looking for someone else to devour (1 Peter 5:8). Though we must remain on guard and alert against the devil, he has been defeated. Jesus has completely shattered all his plans and evil plots. The devil can no longer accuse you before God of your sins, and because of the redemption that is ours in Jesus, we are empowered by the Holy Spirit to resist his temptations.

From the very beginning, God was already at war on our behalf with the devil. The first promise of the coming Savior is recorded in Genesis when God spoke to the devil after Adam and Eve had fallen into sin: "I will put enmity between you and the woman, and between your offspring and her offspring; He [Christ] shall bruise your head, and you shall bruise His heel" (Genesis 3:15). Yes, Jesus crushed Satan most ultimately on the cross, and yes, in that act of loving redemption, Jesus' heel was bruised, indeed, His entire body was horribly tormented, tortured, and killed for us as He utterly destroyed Satan's plots and plans for us. The apostle John explains, "The reason the Son of God appeared was to destroy the works of the devil" (1 John 3:8). James urges us, therefore, in light of Christ's defeat of Satan, to "resist the devil, and he will flee from you" (James 4:7).

What exactly did Jesus provide as the ransom for our sin? Peter writes, "You were ransomed from the futile ways inherited from your forefathers, not with perishable things such as silver or gold, but with the precious blood of Christ, like that of a lamb without blemish or spot" (1 Peter 1:18–19). Remember that "with

His wounds we are healed" (Isaiah 53:5). And John explains that it is "the blood of Jesus His Son" (1 John 1:7) that has cleansed us from all sin. Jesus bled out His lifeblood, gave up His body to the agony of the cross, and offered up His life of perfect obedience, all as the great and final substitute and sacrifice for your sin and mine.

Here's the bottom line for you. Jesus is your substitute. He has atoned for each and every one of our sins and the sins of the whole world. He took your place under God's wrath and judgment. By offering Himself up for your sins, He paid the debt you owed God. We refer to this as the "vicarious satisfaction" or the "vicarious atonement." Watch out for any Christian teacher, preacher, or church that does not clearly proclaim the vicarious satisfaction and atonement of Christ. They are not giving you the Good News! The Good News is that "For our sake He [God] made Him [Christ] to be sin who knew no sin, so that in Him we might become the righteousness of God" (2 Corinthians 5:21).

Is the atonement of Christ limited only to a certain group or type of person? No. Wouldn't it be horrible if it were? What kind of good news would that be? "Hey, Jesus died for sins, but not for yours, or not for theirs." No, Jesus clearly "died for all" (2 Corinthians 5:15). And in 2 Corinthians 5:19, Paul makes it very clear that "In Christ God was reconciling the world to Himself, not counting their trespasses against them." "The world" means . . . the world. If we were left in doubt about any part of what the "world" means, what a horrible doubt and torment that would be! Let us conclude this presentation on the redemption of Christ with a beautiful statement by Paul. Make it your own! "The saying is trustworthy and deserving of full acceptance, that Christ Jesus came into the world to save sinners, of whom I am the foremost" (1 Timothy 1:15).

How God Applies the Atonement to You Personally

It is one thing to know and understand what Christ' work of redemption is and what the atonement is all about, but how does God actually give you the benefit of Christ's saving work on your behalf? How do you receive it? How does God

TECHNICAL STUFF

Vicarious means "substitute." **Satisfaction** is to "fulfill the requirements and conditions for something to happen." And so when we refer to the "vicarious satisfaction" of Christ, that phrase is shorthand for saying that Jesus Christ is our substitute before God, who takes the punishment our sins deserve and satisfies the perfect will and commands of God for us, in our place, on our behalf.

NEED TO KNOW

Means of Grace. The means by which God gives us the forgiveness, life, and salvation won by the death and resurrection of Christ: God's Word, Absolution, Baptism, and the Lord's Supper.

apply it to you, personally? He does it through what we call the "Means of Grace," that is, the Word of the Gospel and the Sacraments by which God the Holy Spirit promises to be active and present in your life, applying the grace of God to you, earned for you by the work of Christ.

How can we explain how God uses these means to convey to us the benefits of Christ's perfect life, atoning passion and death, and victorious resurrection? Imagine the work of Christ as a huge nuclear reactor filled with the energy of God's grace, mercy, and forgiving love and kindness toward humankind. It burns with unimaginable strength and power. But how would anyone ever benefit from all that energy unless there were a system of power lines connecting each person to the power plant of God's love? The Means of Grace serve that purpose. They are, so to speak, the power lines God uses to connect each of us to His mercy.

And so, whenever we hear the Gospel read, preached, or taught, or when we ourselves meditate on it, the Holy Spirit is pouring into us the saving benefits of Christ's work. Baptism is the action by which God buries us with Christ into His death and raises us to new life. "We were buried therefore with Him by baptism into death, in order that, just as Christ was raised from the dead by the glory of the Father, we too might walk in newness of life" (Romans 6:4). When the pastor speaks the word of Christ's forgiveness to us, either in a group, or individually, we know that Christ has so blessed and commissioned this speaking of His Word that it conveys His forgiveness: "If you forgive the sins of any, they are forgiven them; if you withhold forgiveness from any, it is withheld" (John 20:23). And when we receive the body and blood of Christ in the Lord's Supper, we receive the very body and blood that paid for the sins of the whole world and which are being conveyed to us from the altar and in our mouths. Indeed, it is as Christ promises: "This is My body, given for you. This is My blood, shed for you, for the forgiveness of sins."

We do not need to go looking for a "special experience" or constantly work ourselves up into some special kind of spiritual emotion or frenzy. God has given us His Means of Grace, and we can be sure and certain that, just as He has promised, the Holy Spirit is at work through them to sustain us in the faith, to strengthen us through the forgiveness of sins, and to fill us with His power for life by His name, by His mercy.

Passion Week Map and Explanation

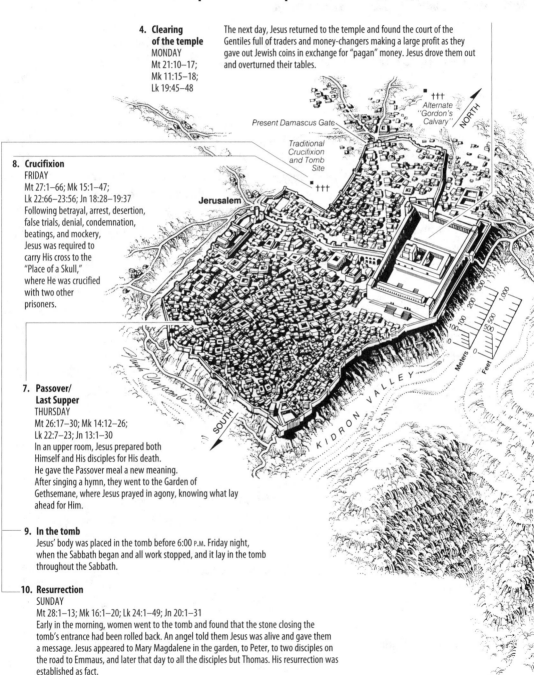

4. Clearing of the temple
MONDAY
Mt 21:10–17;
Mk 11:15–18;
Lk 19:45–48

The next day, Jesus returned to the temple and found the court of the Gentiles full of traders and money-changers making a large profit as they gave out Jewish coins in exchange for "pagan" money. Jesus drove them out and overturned their tables.

Present Damascus Gate

Alternate "Gordon's Calvary"

Traditional Crucifixion and Tomb Site

NORTH

†††

†††

Jerusalem

8. Crucifixion
FRIDAY
Mt 27:1–66; Mk 15:1–47;
Lk 22:66–23:56; Jn 18:28–19:37
Following betrayal, arrest, desertion, false trials, denial, condemnation, beatings, and mockery, Jesus was required to carry His cross to the "Place of a Skull," where He was crucified with two other prisoners.

SOUTH

KIDRON VALLEY

Meters

Feet

7. Passover/ Last Supper
THURSDAY
Mt 26:17–30; Mk 14:12–26;
Lk 22:7–23; Jn 13:1–30
In an upper room, Jesus prepared both Himself and His disciples for His death. He gave the Passover meal a new meaning. After singing a hymn, they went to the Garden of Gethsemane, where Jesus prayed in agony, knowing what lay ahead for Him.

9. In the tomb
Jesus' body was placed in the tomb before 6:00 P.M. Friday night, when the Sabbath began and all work stopped, and it lay in the tomb throughout the Sabbath.

10. Resurrection
SUNDAY
Mt 28:1–13; Mk 16:1–20; Lk 24:1–49; Jn 20:1–31
Early in the morning, women went to the tomb and found that the stone closing the tomb's entrance had been rolled back. An angel told them Jesus was alive and gave them a message. Jesus appeared to Mary Magdalene in the garden, to Peter, to two disciples on the road to Emmaus, and later that day to all the disciples but Thomas. His resurrection was established as fact.

PUTTING IT ALL TOGETHER

The Crucifixion of Jesus Christ

by Dr. Gerard Joseph Stanley Sr., M.D.

The cross in early Christianity was not the symbol of salvation that it has become today. Instead, it was a highly offensive symbol that imposed a tremendous burden on the earliest preachers of Christ and the faith. Crucifixion was a form of capital punishment generally reserved for slaves, traitors, deserters, and revolutionaries, among whom Jesus was numbered. His death by crucifixion implied that Christ was a criminal, not a king; a revolutionary, not the Savior; a slave, not a ruler. As Paul states, the cross was a scandal and an offense. As far as the archaeological evidence indicates, imagery of Jesus crucified or of the cross was not helpful or appealing in the Early Church's mission of proclaiming Christ as the Savior of the world. It was not until the fifth and sixth centuries that the crucifix became a symbol of the Christian faith. The earliest crucifixes depicted Jesus not as a suffering and reviled man, but standing in front of the cross with arms stretched toward heaven. He was pictured in His glory. Not until several centuries later is Jesus depicted in the fullness of His Passion and death—as a man who was crucified on a cross.

What actually happens to a person's body in the process of dying on a cross? How did Jesus suffer? How cruel was the experience of crucifixion?

At Golgotha (Skull Place), the site of execution, Jesus was offered a mixture of wine and myrrh called gall. This bitter mixture traditionally was offered as a mild analgesic to dull the senses before the act of crucifixion. Today, gall would be equivalent to a weak mixture of acetaminophen in a wine solution. Once this mixture touched His lips, Jesus refused to drink it. More ceremonial than effective, gall would have done little to relieve the pain that followed.

Upon arriving at Golgotha, Jesus was thrown on top of the *patibulum*, which would have been placed on the ground after being carried to the site by Simon. This action would have forced dirt into the wounds on Jesus' back, head, and legs, causing the blood to coagulate, harden, and dry. The crown of thorns would have been forced deeper into His scalp, creating more intense pain and further bleeding.

The cross height, as well as its design, have been debated for centuries. As indicated earlier, the tau cross (*crux humulis*), or low cross, which resembles a capital *T*, was used most commonly in that region of the Roman Empire. A Latin cross (*crux sublimis*), which was taller and shaped like a lowercase *t*, would have required special preparation. Because the crucifixion of Jesus was not planned and followed trials and a verdict rendered in just a few short hours, the fixed upright *stipes* of Golgotha would most likely have been employed in this hasty situation.

The *stipes* has been estimated to be approximately six or seven feet in height. At this height, the *patibulum* could be affixed quite easily to the *stipes*, and the feet would have been approximately one foot off the ground. Thus the feet of the victim could have been easily attached to the *stipes* with only a slight bend of the legs—an easy task for the Roman detail. The victim's mouth would have hung at a level even with or slightly lower than the level of the *patibulum*, approximately seven feet off the ground.

When Jesus said, "I thirst," He was offered a drink on a sponge. Most likely this drink was *posca*, a sour wine mixed with water (and perhaps egg), a drink common to Roman soldiers. The Roman soldier's short javelin was approximately three feet long, with a metal spear tip adding another foot to the overall length. When held at arm's length, the javelin with the sponge attached would have reached approximately seven feet into the air from the ground.

For many years, exegetes and scientists alike have argued about the method and placement of the nails or spikes used to affix Christ's arms and legs to the cross. Many exegetes believe Jesus' arms were suspended with nails driven through His hands. In 1953, P. Barbet conducted an experiment in which he tied weights on cadaver arms to determine if using a nail through the web spaces of the hand, between the wrist bones, or elsewhere could hold the weight of a crucified man. He determined that the division of weight between two oblique and symmetrical forces means that each point is bearing considerably more than half of the total weight. Thus nails placed into the hands would need to hold firmly in place and support the equivalent of nearly 240 pounds per nail. He concluded that a nail driven through only the soft tissues of the hand would not hold the weight of a man suspended and writhing on a cross. The nail would have been pulled through the full thickness of the hand if it was driven only through these tissues. However, Barbet did conclude that the area between the bones of the wrist and the end of the forearm's radial bone is sufficiently strong to hold the weight of a man during crucifixion. In their studies of anatomy, the Romans considered the wrist to be part of the hand. Thus as the Gospels indicate, the nails would have been driven through the wrists (considered as part of the hand).

The spike or nail used to affix the victim to the cross would have been five to seven inches in length with a square shaft about three-eighths of an inch in diameter. It would have been slightly thinner, but longer, than a modern railroad spike. Most likely the edges of the shaft would have been squared off.

The placement of these spikes was intended to pass through, or crush, the nerves without disrupting the blood vessels. At the top of the palm, there is a crease formed when bringing the thumb and the little finger together. This crease is at the junction of the short muscles of the thumb and the little finger. Behind this ridge and approximately one-inch wide is a thick, fibrous ligament connected to the bones on the little finger side and to the bones on the thumb side. This transverse carpal ligament forms a tunnel at the wrist to protect the median nerve that connects to the thumb, fingers, and hand. The median nerve is the primary sensory and motor nerve of the hand and most of the fingers. The release of this ligament today is commonly referred to as carpal tunnel release. Bringing the thumb and little finger together creates a hollow, or soft spot, just above the carpal ligament at the main folding line of the wrist. This hollow area, referred to as Destot's space, allows easy access for placing a nail through the wrist bones. Passing a nail through this space would not break any bones and would provide full weight-bearing ability to the carpal ligament. The nail would have crushed, or partially severed, the median nerve, causing intense and continuous pain. Crushing the median nerve would have caused the thumb to flex in toward the palm of the hand and created a clawlike contraction of the index, long, and ring fingers. With the squared-off spikes holding the arms in place, the continuous pain from the crushed median nerve would have intensified with any movement of the arms or body.

A nail driven into Destot's space would cause severe pain but would damage only venous structures with very slow blood loss. This is because the arteries of the hand run on both sides of the wrist. After entering the hand, they arch further down in the palm rather than across Destot's space. No damage to arterial blood flow would have occurred from spikes driven into the body in this area. Thus rapid blood loss was avoided, serving to prolong the agony of crucifixion. The Romans were experts at crucifixion and knew how to cause the most pain with the least amount of blood loss, making this the most painful and drawn-out process of humiliation, suffering, and death imaginable.

The possibility of using ropes to hold the arms of the victim to the *patibulum* has been voiced through the years. If the nails or spikes were placed correctly, there would be no need for ropes tied around the *patibulum* to support the arms. If the nails were placed in an area that would not hold the weight of a crucified man, then ropes would be necessary to keep the victim affixed to the cross. There is no mention in the Scriptures of ropes being used, so it is assumed that Jesus did not have ropes to support Him.

Jesus' arms would have been affixed to the cross with a little bend at His elbows because this, too, helped prolong the suffering.

As was proven in horrific studies in concentration camps during the Second World War, the Romans knew that if the arms were affixed straight or directly above the victim, he would die more quickly. Since the inability to breathe correctly is the main cause of death during crucifixion, the slight bend in the elbows allowed the victim to adjust his chest configuration and continue to breathe, thus prolonging the suffering.

Once Christ's arms were affixed to the *patibulum*, the Roman detail would have picked up the ends of the *patibulum* to affix the crossbeam to the *stipes*. Christ would have been suspended by His wrists while they lifted the crossbeam up and over the top of the *stipes* and dropped it, and Him, into place. The total weight of the *patibulum* and Jesus would not have been more than three hundred and twenty-five pounds. Lifting the crucified victim, as well as the *patibulum*, easily would have been accomplished by an experienced crucifixion detail, especially if the *stipes* was not more than six or seven feet high. The shear agony of this procedure is hard to fathom.

The Romans also knew that the agony of death could be prolonged if the feet were nailed to the cross. If the feet were left to dangle, the victim experienced a hasty death. To prolong the process, the feet were nailed or tied to the *stipes*. The nails placed through the feet had to support the weight of a man while he pushed up to breathe.

Where the feet of the victim were placed on the cross—one on top of the other, side by side, or on each side of the cross—has been a matter of discussion. Barbet and others have postulated that each foot was affixed to its side of the cross. Other scholars feel the feet were nailed one over the other or even separately to the front of the cross. Some have postulated the use of one nail in each foot, regardless of their positioning. The Shroud of Turin reveals a victim with the left foot over the top of the right, implying the use of only one nail.

The nail used to affix the feet would have been the same length as those in the wrists and would have been placed as strategically as they were. Because a key artery moves behind the first long bone of the foot at the top of the arch, the nail would have passed between the second and third long bones. Thus only venous blood, not arterial blood, would have been disrupted.

A nail placed in this area of the body would have passed through or come in contact with the deep nerve (peroneal) of the foot, as well as branches of both the medial and lateral nerves (plantar). A nail placed in Lisfranc's space, which separates the upper foot and ankle bones (tarsals) from the long bones (metatarsals) of the foot, would hold the weight of a man while pushing himself up, but it would not break any bones. The legs would have been slightly bent at the knees to secure the feet to the cross. As with the arms, damage to the nerves of the feet would have created lightning-bolt flashes of pain along the entire length of Jesus' legs. His body weight and any movement around the square nails would intensify the pain.

The Romans used the act of crucifixion as a show of force and a deterrent to crime and rebellion. The victim's body would hang on the cross from hours to days, even after death had occurred. The victims were suspended off the ground on a high point in the city or along a busy road so citizens and those passing by would witness this demonstration of force and intimidation.

Crucifixion was horrifically painful. While hanging on the cross, the victim's full weight was borne by his wrists and feet at the point at which the spikes had been driven through them and into the wood. The greatest impact of crucifixion was on the victim's breathing. When "breathing in," a person normally activates the muscles of the chest and the diaphragm to bring air into the lungs. During exhalation, or "breathing out," a person relaxes the chest muscles and diaphragm and air moves out of the lungs. During crucifixion, this process is essentially reversed. The position of the body on the cross creates an emphysematous, or "barrel-chested," victim, preventing normal airflow in and out of the lungs.

To breathe in and out, Jesus would have to move up and down on the *stipes*. He would have to lift Himself up by pulling on His wrists and pushing up on His feet. With any movement, the spikes driven through His feet would have sent shearing pain up both legs. Likewise, with the movement upward to exhale, His arms would have rotated around the spikes, causing excruciating pain to shoot through His upper body and arms. It is difficult to imagine the agonizing pain. Each breath would have forced Jesus to push up on His feet, push His back against the *stipes*, and rotate His arms on the *patibulum*. His back, with its shredded flesh and muscle, would have grated against the rough timber. With each breath, each movement against the cross would have caused excruciating pain throughout the body and pushed the thorns ever deeper into His scalp. Jesus eventually would have tired of holding Himself in the fully extended breathing position and would have sagged into the crucified position. Yet to breathe, Jesus would have to repeat this agonizing process. Exhaustion soon followed.

In a feeble attempt to temporarily relieve the severe muscle cramps and progressive reversal of normal heart and kidney function, Jesus would have tried to restore His breathing to a more normal pattern, thus realigning the blood flow in His extremities. In an effort to exhale the life-draining carbon dioxide and inhale fresh life-saving oxygen, Jesus would have pushed up on His feet, rotated His arms around the squared nails, and pulled His body up on the cross. From the spikes, shearing pain would have shot up both legs with any movement. The rotation of the arms around the spikes would have caused lightening-like pain through His arms and entire upper body. Each breath would have forced Jesus to push up on His feet, push His back against the *stipes*, and rotate His arms on the *patibulum*. The open sores and the torn flesh and muscle on His back would have grated against the rough timber. Each movement up and down with each breath would have caused excruciating pain over Jesus' back, arms, legs, and head, the crown of thorns pushing ever deeper into His flesh. Jesus eventually would have tired of holding Himself in this position, only to sag back down into the crucified, life-ending position.

To continue breathing, Jesus would need to repeat this agonizing, painful, and life-draining process. The crucifixion was spent straightening out His body to exhale, and then slumping down again to inhale. The result was an alternation between attempting to breathe normally and progressive asphyxia. Exhaustion was soon to follow. The only positive in death would have been the cessation of the pain.

Reflecting on the events of the Passion of our Lord Jesus Christ shines light on the man Jesus as He gives Himself unconditionally to His Father. The Father's will is done. In reflecting on the crucifixion, we see Jesus suffer as a man and forgive as the Son of God.

Jesus' crucifixion shows love, understanding, and forgiveness in the face of sinners and sin. Christians trust in the mercy and forgiveness of God in Jesus Christ through His death and resurrection, and we continue the love, understanding, and forgiveness Jesus demonstrated on the cross in our lives of faith.

—From *He Was Crucified; Reflections on the Passion of Christ*
(St. Louis: Concordia, 2009)

The Meaning and Purpose of the Season of Lent

From the very earliest years of the Christian Church, the time of what we now refer to as "Holy Week" was at the high point of the Church's year. Tracing the life of Christ during His last days on earth, particularly the night before He was betrayed and the day He was crucified, were the most solemn observations in the Church's year. These holy days prepared the people of God for a joyful celebration of Jesus' resurrection on Easter Sunday. As time went on, to offer people a special number of weeks to prepare for the holiest of days and the great Easter celebration, the Church developed a six-week period known as Lent. The word *Lent* derives from the Old English word for spring. The season roughly corresponds each year to the change of seasons, from winter to spring.

During the forty-day period of Lent, it is common for Christians to attend special midweek worship services, to engage in a series of special readings and prayers in private and family devotions, and to fast, that is, to abstain from the normal quantity of food consumed during the day. This is all done to focus hearts and minds on our need for a Savior and to help us meditate deeply on that need and come to a deeper appreciation and love for the Savior who came to suffer and die for us.

In the Early Church, Holy Week was the high point for those seeking to become Christians. They would go through a careful period of instruction and examination. Then, where possible, they would be baptized on Saturday night before Easter Sunday, literally arising from the waters of their Baptism at the stroke of midnight. They would be ushered into the full worshiping community that would be aglow with candles and lamps and greeted joyfully with the ancient Easter greeting, "Christ is risen! He is risen indeed!"

In most Lutheran congregations today, there are midweek worship services, often organized around a particular theme or topic. It is not uncommon for Lutheran congregations to use the six weeks in Lent to review the six chief parts of Luther's Small Catechism. At the conclusion of the series of midweek services, Holy Week is observed with special worship services on Thursday night, Friday, and Friday night, and in some congregations, a "vigil" service on Saturday night, and then Easter services, either early morning or later in the morning or often both. The series of worship services in Holy Week culminating on Easter Sunday is known as the "triduum" or "three days," beginning on Holy Thursday evening, also known as Maundy Thursday, through the evening of Easter Sunday.

In Lent, we are permitted a special opportunity every year to remember the great events of Christ's sacrificial life and death for us, to walk along the road that led our Savior to the cross, and then to rejoice together in the empty tomb and resurrection of Jesus.

Study Questions

1. Read Exodus 12:7–13; 24:5–8; Matthew 26:26–29. What is the significance of blood in these passages?

2. What does it mean to be a slave to sin? See Romans 6:20. What hope do you have of being freed from your sin?

3. What happens in Holy Baptism?

4. How do you receive the benefits of Christ's saving work in His death and resurrection?

5. What is the purpose of Lent?

Visit lutheranism101.com to download the free Leader Guide.

Discussion Questions

1. What consequences of sin do you see in the world and in your own life? What consequences of Christ's payment for your sin do you see in the world and in your own life?

2. Dwell on this fact: You are the reason God's Son, Jesus Christ, humbled Himself and became man. Why did He do this? What does the truth of that statement mean to you?

3. Many Christians believe their Baptism is an act they make either for Jesus or as a profession of their faith. How does the Lutheran understanding of Baptism differ? How is Christ's death and resurrection linked to Holy Baptism?

4. As a Christian, you have received the most precious treasure on earth: the Gospel of forgiveness. If you have received such a wonderful gift, why is it so hard to share it with others? Think of a time when you felt you could never forgive someone.

Visit lutheranism101.com to download the free Leader Guide.

CHAPTER 9

The State of Exaltation

In This Chapter

- Christ descended into hell.
- Jesus rose from the dead—body and all.
- He's gone, always among us, and coming back again.

Crucified, died, and was buried. If Jesus' story ended there, we would be, as Paul says, "most to be pitied" (1 Corinthians 15:19). If the work of Christ only included His humiliation, it would have been a very sad story indeed and we

MAKING CONNECTIONS

What do other world religions and cults believe about Jesus?

Islam: Jesus is one of the prophets sent by God, with Muhammad being the last and greatest prophet of God. It is blasphemy to teach that Jesus is the Son of God.

Judaism: If Jesus existed at all, He was a religious teacher, perhaps mentally unbalanced, but not the promised Messiah.

Hinduism: Jesus may be one of the many manifestations of the divine. Some Hindus think Jesus is one of the many incarnations of the god Vishnu.

Buddhism: If they say anything at all about Jesus, Buddhists regard Him as a good man and wise teacher of moral truths.

Mormonism: Jesus was conceived by a sexual act before the creation of the world between the Father and Mary. They regard Jesus as Son of God but not equal to the Father. Mormonism uses many words and phrases from Christianity but packs them with meanings that contradict the Bible.

Jehovah's Witness: They regard Jesus to be secondary to the Father, and are modern-day Arians who believe that Jesus is not of one substance with the Father. They do not worship Jesus and reject biblical Christianity.

would merely all admire a great man, referring to Him as a "spiritual leader." But the story of Jesus does not end with His death and burial. From the depths of utter humiliation and degradation, for our salvation, Christ was exalted. In this section, we will review the steps along the path of His exaltation, including His "victory lap" through hell, His resurrection, His appearances after His resurrection, His ascension, and His presence now for all eternity at the right hand of God the Father. He will return again to judge both those still living and all those who are dead.

So, let's trace Christ's walk "up the ladder" of His exaltation as we have it in the Apostles' Creed:

Ladder of Christ's Exaltation

> Comes to judge the living and the dead
>
> Ascended into heaven
>
> Rose again from the dead
>
> He descended into hell

Earlier we discussed how, during His earthly ministry, Christ did not fully use the powers He had as the divine Son of God. The exaltation of Christ is just the opposite: in full glory and power and might, the risen Lord demonstrates the extent of His divine powers. You can catch the joy and awe in Paul's description of the exalted Lord and Savior in Philippians 2:9–11: "God has highly exalted Him and bestowed on Him the name that is above every name, so that at the name of Jesus every knee should bow, in heaven and on earth and under the earth, and every tongue confess that Jesus Christ is Lord, to the glory of God the Father."

NEED TO KNOW

exaltation: The resumption and continuation of such full and constant use of His divine attributes according to His human nature was and is the exaltation of Christ (Ephesians 4:8; Hebrews 2:7).

NEED TO KNOW

In 2 Peter 3:19, "prison" designates the abode of lost souls and evil angels. It is to these that Christ proclaimed His victory (2 Peter 2:4).

Taking a Victory Lap in Hell

It comes as a bit of surprise to many that Christ's descent into hell is counted as one step along the path of His exaltation. For that matter, the idea that Christ at some point after His bodily resurrection and before His appearances on that

NEED TO KNOW

apostle. From the Greek word *apostolos*, meaning "to send." The one sent goes with the full authority of the sender. The apostles were called and sent directly by Jesus.

first Easter Sunday morning entered hell may be a source of confusion and speculation. In the Church, there have been various theories about what exactly happened. Did Christ go to hell to give Satan the ultimate beating? No, that happened on the cross and ended when Christ said, "It is finished." He did not say, "It is finished for now, but watch out, devil! I'm coming and hell's coming with Me this time!" No.

Ultimately, what we can say with assurance based on the Bible is that Christ did descend into hell, not to suffer further torture and torment for our sins, but rather, to proclaim His victory over His enemies in hell. Talk about the ultimate victory parade! Peter puts it this way, "[Christ was] put to death in the flesh but made alive in the spirit, in which He went and proclaimed to the spirits in prison" (1 Peter 3:18–19). And in Colossians 2:15, Paul writes, "He disarmed the rulers and authorities and put them to open shame, by triumphing over them."

One hymn writer put it this way, "The foe was triumphant when on Calvary the Lord of creation was nailed to the tree. . . . But short was their triumph, the Savior arose; and death, hell and Satan, He vanquished His foes" (*LSB* 480:2–3). You can almost imagine Jesus wiping the smug look off Satan and all His evil minions in hell. Satan, of course, is the one who so audaciously had actually tried to tempt Christ to renounce His mission and receive all earthly power that Satan tried to claim as his!

The Bodily Resurrection of Christ

Of course, the most spectacular event as far as we are concerned is the great and glorious bodily resurrection of Jesus from the grave. On the third day, that is, counting Friday, Saturday, and then Sunday, Christ rose in victory from the grave and revealed Himself to His disciples and many others during the time between His resurrection and His ascension. It is because of the resurrection that Christianity is what it is to this day. Anyone can die. Everyone dies. But only the One who rose bodily over the grave, into which He had voluntarily entered, is the One who has destroyed death and the grave, for He and He alone is the God-man, our great "God With Us," Immanuel, true God of gods and the Son of the Virgin.

Luke records Peter's words in Acts 10:40–41: "God raised Him on the third day and made Him to appear, not to all the people but to us who had been chosen by

God as witnesses, who ate and drank with Him after He rose from the dead." And Paul writes of His personal encounter with the risen Savior,

> He was raised on the third day in accordance with the Scriptures, and . . . He appeared to Cephas [Peter], then to the twelve. Then He appeared to more than five hundred brothers at one time, most of them who are still alive, though some have fallen asleep. Then He appeared to James, then to all the apostles. Last of all, as to one untimely born, He appeared also to me. (1 Corinthians 15:4–8)

Luke, the doctor and historian, begins the Book of Acts with this assertion: "He [Christ] presented Himself alive to them after His suffering by many proofs, appearing to them during forty days and speaking about the kingdom of God" (Acts 1:3).

Each of the four Gospels offers its own unique take on the resurrection. Some people claim that differences amongst the Gospels are proof that they are not trustworthy. But ask yourself this. Does every eyewitness to an event have the exact same word-for-word account? You would be justifiably suspicious if they did! No, each eyewitness has his or her own take on a given event. So in the four Gospels we are privileged to have the words the Holy Spirit desired each writer to share, based on his direct and personal experience with the risen Christ. The four accounts are in Matthew 27:62–28:20; Mark 16; Luke 24; and John 20–21. Read each of these accounts for a rich encounter with the risen Christ for yourself, based on the eyewitness testimonies of the apostles. In fact, a criterion for being an apostle is to be one who personally, directly, and immediately was chosen by Christ to be an eyewitness authoritative teacher for the Church.

> **WHAT DOES THIS MEAN?**
>
> On the Last Day He will raise me and all the dead and give eternal life to me and all believers in Christ. This is most certainly true. (SC, Third Article)

What Does the Resurrection Prove?

It's wonderful that Jesus rose from the dead. But what does it mean? It is understandable that often Christians are left a bit puzzled about the connection between the work of Jesus during His life and the events of His last days before His death and then His resurrection. Let's look at what the Bible teaches us about why the resurrection is so important and comforting.

First, it proves that Christ is the Son of God. Romans 1:4 says, "[He] was declared to be the Son of God in power according to the Spirit of holiness by His resurrection from the dead."

Second, the resurrection proves that Jesus' teachings are all true. He said, "Destroy this temple, and in three days I will raise it up" (John 2:19). John notes that Jesus was referring not to the temple building but rather to His own body. In John 8:28, we read Jesus' words, "When you have lifted up the Son of Man, then you will know that I am He, and that I do nothing on my own authority, but speak just as the Father has taught Me."

Third, it proves that God the Father accepted Christ's sacrifice for the sins of the whole world. In fact, rightly has it been said that resurrection of Christ is the world's absolution. Romans 4:25 states, "[Christ] was delivered up for our trespasses and raised for our justification," and Paul says in Romans 5:10, "If while we were enemies [with God] we were reconciled to God by the death of His Son, much more, now that we are reconciled, shall we be saved by His life." The resurrection is not simply "icing on the cake." It is key to the entire Christian faith, for, "If Christ has not been raised, your faith is futile and you are still in your sins" (1 Corinthians 15:17).

Fourth, the resurrection of Christ proves that all believers in Christ will be raised to eternal life themselves. Jesus promises, "I am the resurrection and the life. Whoever believes in Me, though he die, yet shall he live, and everyone who lives and believes in Me shall never die" (John 11:25–26). He also proclaimed, "Because I live, you also will live" (John 14:19). Paul assures us, "In fact Christ has been raised from the dead, the firstfruits of those who have fallen asleep" (1 Corinthians 15:20).

The Comfort of Christ's Ascension

Christ was not only raised from the dead, but He also ascended bodily into heaven. Forty days after His resurrection, Christ gathered His apostles together and ascended bodily into the sky until clouds removed Him from their sight. The apostles were, no doubt, left with their mouths hanging open, just staring up, to the point that the angels have to basically shoo them back into the city of Jerusalem, where ten days later they were filled with power from God on the great day of Pentecost. What do we know about the ascension and what does it mean for us? (You can read the entire account of Christ's ascension in Acts 1:9–11.)

First, we know Christ offered His Church His final blessing on earth, for "while He blessed them, He parted from them and was carried up into heaven" (Luke 24:51). Paul writes about the

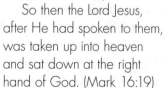

FROM THE BIBLE

So then the Lord Jesus, after He had spoken to them, was taken up into heaven and sat down at the right hand of God. (Mark 16:19)

ascension that "He who descended is the one who also ascended far above all the heavens" (Ephesians 4:10). Jesus ascended but did not go to some other world or into orbit around the earth. We need to remember that He is the one through whom all things that were made have been made. He ascended completely out of this time and space into the realm of heaven, which is not in this time, place, or space. With His incarnated body, He now inhabits His rightful place at God's right hand.

Second, as a result of His ascension, Christ is able to fulfill His promise to us: "In My Father's house are many rooms. If it were not so, would I have told you that I go to prepare a place for you? And if I go and prepare a place for you, I will come again and will take you to Myself, that where I am you may be also" (John 14:2–3). Jesus prayed for us before His crucifixion, "Father, I desire that they also, whom You have given Me, may be with Me where I am, to see My glory" (John 17:24).

Christians have been confessing for two thousand years that Christ has ascended and is now "at the right hand of God." The first Christian martyr, Steven, was given a vision in which He saw this (Acts 7:55–56). In Romans 8, Paul writes that "Christ is the one . . . who is at the right hand of God, who is indeed interceding for us (v. 34). What then does this actually mean? Is there literally a seat at the right hand of God? For that matter, does God the Father have a literal right hand? No, but He has chosen to reveal an image in which this is seen. The truth of Christ's ascension is portrayed for us in this way to teach us what the ascension means. It means that Christ, with both His divine and human natures, now exists for all eternity as a member of the Holy Trinity in that realm we call heaven.

Here is how this reality is explained by Paul in Ephesians 1:20–23:

> He [God] raised Him [Christ] from the dead and seated Him at His right hand in the heavenly places, far above all rule and authority and power and dominion, and above every name that is named, not only in this age but also in the one to come. And He put all things under His feet and gave Him as head over all things to the church, which is His body, the fullness of Him who fills all in all.

BELIEVE, TEACH, CONFESS

He ascended into heaven to sit at the right hand of the Father. There He forever reigns and has dominion over all creatures. He sanctifies those who believe in Him, by sending the Holy Spirit into their hearts to rule, comfort, and make them alive. He defends them against the devil and the power of sin. (AC III 4–5)

Note particularly the last statement that Christ "fills all in all." The capacity of human language fails to adequately explain precisely where and what heaven is. We should not speculate beyond the limits of our human reason but accept in faith what has been revealed. Christ Jesus, as the eternal God-man in light of the incarnation, now fills all things in glory and might.

Why is it such a powerful comfort and blessing to know this? We know that the fully exalted God-man, Jesus Christ, is forever the Lord of the Church. He, as our last and final Word from God, sends men out to fill the office of the holy ministry that He has given as a gift to the Church for the purpose of proclaiming the Good News of salvation and to distribute the Sacraments, all by the power of the Holy Spirit. It is as the apostle Paul describes in Ephesians 4:10–12: "([He] ascended far above all the heavens, that He might fill all things.) And He gave the apostles, the prophets, the evangelists, the shepherd and teachers, to equip the saints for the work of ministry, for building up the body of Christ." Shepherd and teachers or, if you will, "shepherds who teach" are the pastors Christ sends to this very day and hour to equip God's people to serve one another and to help build up the Body of Christ.

Christ Is Always Present Among Us

The promise Christ gives to those who are called and ordained to the pastoral office today is this: "The one who hears you hears Me" (Luke 10:16). This is why our pastors say to us when they absolve sins, "I as a called and ordained servant of the Word, *in the stead and by the command of my Lord Jesus Christ,* forgive you all your sins." They stand in the place of Christ, as His ambassadors. They are not speaking their opinions or their word but the Word of the Lord of the Church, Jesus Christ. And as Jesus explained, it was to our advantage that He ascended, for "If I do not go away, the Helper will not come to you. But if I go, I will send Him to you" (John 16:7). Here Jesus describes the unique work of the Holy Spirit, who through the preaching and teaching of God's Word and the administration of the Sacraments calls, gathers, and enlightens a people for Himself, forming, shaping, and strengthening the Church and each individual member of the Church.

Because of His ascension, we are comforted to know that Jesus, as the Great High Priest, continues His priestly work of praying for His Church. Romans 8:34 assures of the ongoing intercession of Christ for His Church. First John 2:1 promises us that "If anyone does sin, we have an advocate with the Father, Jesus Christ the righteous." And as our everlasting King, Jesus always rules and protects His Church and governs the whole world for the express benefit of His Church. We cannot explain why things happen the way they happen, but we have God's promise that all things are in accord with His good and gracious will for His Church.

We are assured that as He ascended, Christ will come again at the end of this present age. He will return visibly and with great glory on the great and final Last Day. Jesus Himself said, "As the lightning comes from the east and shines as far as the west, so will be the coming of the Son of Man" (Matthew 24:27). Luke records Jesus' words, "Then they will see the Son of Man coming in a cloud with power and great glory" (Luke 21:27). On the day of His ascension, the angels told His apostles, "Men of Galilee, why do you stand looking into heaven? This Jesus, who was taken up from you into heaven, will come in the same way as you saw Him go into heaven" (Acts 1:11). Peter teaches this about the coming of Christ: "The day of the Lord will come like a thief, and then the heavens will pass away with a roar, and the heavenly bodies will be burned up and dissolved, and the earth and the works that are done on it will be exposed" (2 Peter 3:10). And in Revelation 1:7, we read, "Behold, He is coming with the clouds, and every eye will see Him, even those who pierced Him, and all the tribes of the earth will wail on account of Him. Even so. Amen."

NEED TO KNOW

Last Day or Judgment Day. The day of Christ's return, which will also be the end of the world and the bodily resurrection of all mankind. Christ the judge, who knows all things, will proceed at once to pronounce sentence by judicial and final separation. Believers (righteous) will be awarded the everlasting kingdom prepared for them by Him as an inheritance (Galatians 3:26–29). The unbelievers (unrighteous) will be condemned to everlasting punishment (Matthew 25:24–46).

He's Coming Back!

Christ is returning one day, on the Last Day, to judge the world, not to set up or establish some new earthly government or "millennial kingdom" or any other such fantasy. Such speculations and theories and teachings have no basis in Holy Scripture but represent dangerous false doctrine because they lead people to the inevitable conclusion that there is some grand "second chance" to turn in trust to the Savior. No, the Scriptures make clear that God says, "In a favorable time I listened to you, and in a day of salvation I have helped you." Behold, now is the favorable time; behold, now is the day of salvation" (2 Corinthians 6:2). The Last Day is truly the end of this world as we know it. Jesus says, "When the Son of Man comes in His glory, and all the angels with Him, then He will sit on His glorious throne. Before Him will be gathered all the nations, and He will separate people one from another as a shepherd separates the sheep from the goats" (Matthew 25:31–32). And in John 12, we read, "The one who rejects Me and does not receive My words has a judge; the word that I have spoken will judge him on the last day" (v. 48). The final judgment is described in more detail in Matthew 25:31–46.

False Teachings Concerning the Second Coming of Christ

We should note at this point that a teaching called "millennialism" would have us believe that either before or after Christ's return the Church will experience a literal thousand-year period of time that will be an unprecedented era of peace and prosperity here on earth for the Church. This false teaching is based on a fundamental misunderstanding of Revelation 20, which speaks in highly figurative language about the spiritual rule of Christ through the Church's ministry of Word and Sacrament. Contrary to what millennialists believe, Revelation 20 does not refer to a literal earthly government or kingdom.

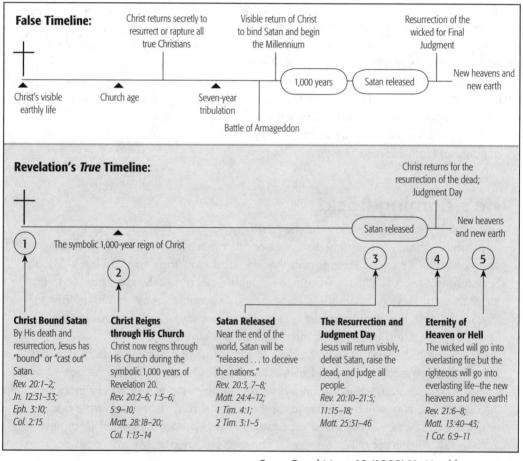

False Timeline:

Christ returns secretly to resurrect or rapture all true Christians

Visible return of Christ to bind Satan and begin the Millennium

Resurrection of the wicked for Final Judgment

1,000 years   Satan released

New heavens and new earth

Christ's visible earthly life

Church age

Seven-year tribulation

Battle of Armageddon

Revelation's *True* Timeline:

Christ returns for the resurrection of the dead; Judgment Day

Satan released

New heavens and new earth

The symbolic 1,000-year reign of Christ

1 Christ Bound Satan
By His death and resurrection, Jesus has "bound" or "cast out" Satan.
Rev. 20:1–2;
Jn. 12:31–33;
Eph. 3:10;
Col. 2:15

2 Christ Reigns through His Church
Christ now reigns through His Church during the symbolic 1,000 years of Revelation 20.
Rev. 20:2–6; 1:5–6;
5:9–10;
Matt. 28:18–20;
Col. 1:13–14

Satan Released
Near the end of the world, Satan will be "released . . . to deceive the nations."
Rev. 20:3, 7–8;
Matt. 24:4–12;
1 Tim. 4:1;
2 Tim. 3:1–5

3 The Resurrection and Judgment Day
Jesus will return visibly, defeat Satan, raise the dead, and judge all people.
Rev. 20:10–21:5;
11:15–18;
Matt. 25:31–46

4 5 Eternity of Heaven or Hell
The wicked will go into everlasting fire but the righteous will go into everlasting life–the new heavens and new earth!
Rev. 21:6–8;
Matt. 13:40–43;
1 Cor. 6:9–11

—From *Good News* 12 (1999):11. Used by permission.

Be Ready!

What Christ wants us to do to prepare for His second coming is "be ready" because "the Son of Man is coming at an hour you do not expect" (Matthew 24:44). Remember that during His earthly ministry, Christ humbled Himself and refrained from the full exercise of His divine powers and abilities. No better example of this could be found than in this assertion Jesus made during His state of humiliation: "Concerning that day or that hour, no one knows, not even the angels in heaven, nor the Son, but only the Father" (Mark 13:32). And when Paul spoke to the cultural elites of the center of Greco-Roman culture in Athens, he said, "[God] has fixed a day on which He will judge the world in righteousness by a man whom He has appointed" (Acts 17:31). During His life, Jesus taught constantly about His return and continually urges us, His followers, to remain watchful and waiting. See, for example, His parable about the wise and foolish virgins in Matthew 25:1–13.

What can we as God's people expect before the return of Christ? Frankly, exactly what Jesus said we should expect: "Nation will rise against nation, and kingdom against kingdom, and there will be famines and earthquakes in various places" (Matthew 24:7). But you may say, "This happens all the time!" Precisely the point. Take these events that are ongoing as warning signals that this world as we know it is not permanent, not eternal, not a lasting city for us to dwell in. Christ warns us, "If those days had not been cut short, no human being would be saved. But for the sake of the elect those days will be cut short" (Matthew 24:22). And the most dangerous thing that will continue to increase as we move closer to the Last Day is a falling away from the faith and people gathering around false teachers

FROM THE BIBLE

Then the kingdom of heaven will be like ten virgins who took their lamps and went to meet the bridegroom. Five of them were foolish, and five were wise. For when the foolish took their lamps, they took no oil with them, but the wise took flasks of oil with their lamps. As the bridegroom was delayed, they all became drowsy and slept. But at midnight there was a cry, "Here is the bridegroom! Come out to meet him." Then all those virgins rose and trimmed their lamps. And the foolish said to the wise, "Give us some of your oil, for our lamps are going out." But the wise answered, saying, "Since there will not be enough for us and for you, go rather to the dealers and buy for yourselves." And while they were going to buy, the bridegroom came, and those who were ready went in with him to the marriage feast, and the door was shut. Afterward the other virgins came also, saying, "Lord, lord, open to us." But he answered, "Truly, I say to you, I do not know you." Watch therefore, for you know neither the day nor the hour. (Matthew 25:1–13) and false prophets. "The Spirit expressly says that in later times some will depart from the faith by devoting themselves to deceitful spirits and teachings of demons" (1 Timothy 4:1). You can read a more complete accounting of things that will happen in that time immediately before Christ does return in Matthew 24.

Christians need to be aware that following Jesus is not some kind of way to avoid trouble or danger or persecution or all the other troubles that we know come directly as a result of being a follower of Jesus. Any preacher or teacher who tries to tell you that the key to "prosperity" and "success" and "wealth" is following Jesus, he or she is a false teacher and must be rejected and avoided! Jesus is very clear, and we must also therefore be very clear. Being a Christian is not a path to earthly popularity and success. No, in fact, Jesus offers very sobering words to us. Let's review what He has to say about being His follower before He returns again.

In John 16:1–4, we read Christ's warning: "I have said all these things to you to keep you from falling away. They will put you out of the synagogues. Indeed, the hour is coming when whoever kills you will think he is offering service to God. And they will do these things because they have not known the Father, nor Me. But I have said these things to you, that when their hour comes you may remember that I told them to you." We see that Jesus' words came true as we read through the Book of Acts about the various troubles and hardships the first Christians faced.

But we look forward to the great and Last Day. On that day, those who have fallen asleep in Christ will arise, and those still present will be caught up with Christ in the air. We will receive our new resurrection bodies and forever enjoy, in those new bodies, the new heavens and new earth, where the glory of God and the Lamb of God will provide for us light eternal, in the unending billions of years to come in eternity. What joy awaits is beyond our ability to understand, but we eagerly await it! Thanks be to God!

Study Questions

1. Why is Jesus' resurrection key to the entire Christian faith?

2. What four things does the resurrection prove?

3. Why are these four things important to know and understand?

4. Why did God the Father send the Holy Spirit to His people? What unique work does this third member of the Trinity do?

5. What does God tell us to expect before the return of Christ? See Matthew 24.

6. If such events are not new to us today, what is their purpose?

Visit lutheranism101.com to download the free Leader Guide.

Discussion Questions

1. Read Acts 1:6–11. Pretend you are Luke on the day of Jesus' ascension into heaven. What thoughts would be circling inside of your head?

2. What does Jesus warn His followers about in John 16:1–4? How can we take comfort in the face of trouble and hardship that come our way because of our faith?

3. Non-Christians and even some Christians do not believe in hell or in a God who claims to be loving but also allows people to go to hell. How do we reconcile a loving God with the reality of hell?

Visit lutheranism101.com to download the free Leader Guide.

Conclusion: Why Is Lutheranism All About Jesus?

We've covered a lot of ground in this book. A number of years ago, I was talking to another Christian who was not Lutheran, and she made an interesting observation. She said, "It seems like all you Lutherans talk about is Jesus." The comment caught me off guard and I wanted simply to say, "Well, of course, what else are we supposed to talk about?" But then it struck me that she had put her finger on what is perhaps the greatest crisis in Christendom: a failure to keep Christ and His Good News at the center of everything the Church teaches and preaches and shares with people.

If we rather mindlessly repeat a few key doctrines about Christ without fully preaching the whole counsel of God on all the various things it proclaims, we are not being faithful. On the other hand, how many examples do we find today of Christian churches that allow other issues and emphases to cloud the centrality of the crucified and risen Christ. Be it left or right politics, or the latest social, environmental, or cultural issues, the Christian Church must remain the place where the love and mercy of God in Christ is consistently proclaimed.

The Lutheran Church was born in the midst of a reforming movement in the Church. Since that time the Church has always been, and must always be, in a state of "reformation"— always repenting of sin; receiving God's gifts of forgiveness, life, and salvation delivered through the Word and Sacraments; and boldly proclaiming this Good News. Both "in season and out of season," as Paul says in 2 Timothy 4:2, we preach the Word!

Lutheranism is all about Jesus because Christianity is all about Jesus! If it is not, it is

WHAT DOES THIS MEAN?

I believe that Jesus Christ . . . has redeemed me, a lost and condemned person, purchased and won me from all sins, from death, and from the power of the devil, not with gold or silver, but with His holy, precious blood and with His innocent suffering and death, that I may be His own and live under Him in His kingdom and serve Him in everlasting righteousness. (SC, Second Article) not Christianity, but something else. It may look like Christianity. It may sound like Christianity, but it is not Christianity. Likewise, the further a particular Lutheran church body or congregation drifts away from the truths of God's holy, infallible, and inerrant Word, the further away it drifts from Jesus. And to that extent, it is Lutheran in name only.

Christ has redeemed you. He has called you by name, and you are free to live under Him in His kingdom, as the Small Catechism explains it. You are set free by Jesus Christ from slavery to sin and are freed to serve God by serving your neighbor in love, in whatever calling and station in life you have. The grace of God in Christ transforms you and makes you clean. You are a new person. In Romans 6, Paul puts it this way: "We know that our old self was crucified with Him in order that the body of sin might be brought to nothing, so that we would no longer be enslaved to sin" (v. 6). In 2 Corinthians 5:15, we read, "He [Christ] died for all, that those who live might no longer live for themselves but for Him who for their sake died and was raised." As Paul further explains, "Therefore, as you received Christ Jesus the Lord, so walk in Him, rooted and built up in Him and established in the faith, just as you were taught, abounding in thanksgiving" (Colossians 2:6–7). And in Titus 2, our new life in Christ is described this way: "[Christ] gave Himself for us to redeem us from all lawlessness and to purify for Himself a people for His own possession who are zealous for good works" (v. 14).

As followers of Jesus, our life in Christ is truly all about Him. We serve Him with our whole life here on earth and have the joy of knowing that we will be forever with the Lord in heaven someday. We serve Him "without fear, in holiness and righteousness before Him all our days" (Luke 1:74–75). Peter describes us this way: "You are a chosen race, a royal priesthood, a holy nation, a people for His own possession, that you may proclaim the excellencies of Him who called you out of darkness into His marvelous light" (1 Peter 2:9). We, too, will join the saints who even now are in the presence of Christ in heaven (Revelation 7:13–17). Because Christ is raised from the dead, we then "have been raised with Christ" and therefore are to "seek the things that are above, where Christ is, seated at the right hand of God." We are to set our minds "on things that are above, not on things that are on earth. For you have died, and your life is hidden with Christ in God" (Colossians 3:1–3).

No more beautiful a final statement for this study of Jesus could be found than the words of Paul, who beautifully summarizes why it is all about Jesus. Make these words your own. Ponder them. Meditate on them. Let them accompany you every day.

> I have been crucified with Christ. It is no longer I who live, but Christ who lives in me. And the life I now live in the flesh I live by faith in the Son of God, who loved me and gave Himself for me. (Galatians 2:20)

Christian Meditation: Focusing on Jesus

by John W. Kleinig

There are many different methods of meditation, all equally valid but suited to different persons. From the process of trial and error, we develop our own approach to meditation, discovering how best to enter the contemplative state. The time, place, posture, and routine, things that are not themselves important, may vary from person to person. The method is not what is most important. A Christian, a Buddhist, and a secular psychologist may all employ the same method but with entirely different results. On the other hand, different Christians may use different methods of meditation with similar results.

The key is not how we meditate, but on what we meditate. The object, the focus of meditation, determines what happens to us in our meditation and as a result of our meditation. Our focus grounds and empowers the meditation. Therefore, there is great danger in practicing unfocused forms of meditation, such as totally emptying our minds or repeating a meaningless word. If we practice unfocused meditation, we may indeed enter a contemplative state. But we may then also open ourselves to evil powers that are in us or in the people around us. We may experience something powerful, but it will not be spiritually beneficial for us.

Christian meditation focuses on Christ and His Word. It starts with Jesus and ends with Him. He is the be-all and end-all of Christian meditation. His Word empowers our meditation and determines what happens in it. His Word brings life and light, comfort and health to the soul. We who belong to Him meditate on Him.

The story of Mary and Martha (Luke 10:38–42) teaches us the elements of Christian meditation. Mary is the model for all who meditate. She welcomed Jesus into her house, sat at His feet as His disciple, and listened to His Word.

Her eyes were fixed on Jesus; her ears were attentive to Him; she was open and receptive to Him. Nothing distracted her from Jesus and what He had to say.

Martha stands in contrast to Mary. Whereas Jesus praises Mary, He criticizes Martha. But Jesus does not criticize Martha, as some maintain, for busying herself with the preparation of the meal or for failing to sit at His feet like Mary. Jesus finds fault with her for yielding to anxiety: Martha was annoyed at her sister Mary as she prepared the meal for Him.

Both Mary and Martha were, in fact, engaged in meditation, Mary by listening to Jesus and Martha by cooking the meal for Him. The difference was that Martha lost her focus on Jesus and so missed out on the most needed thing. She was distracted from Him by her anxiety and annoyance. Whether we are activists like Martha or contemplatives like Mary, Jesus must be the focus of our meditation. Everything else is distraction.

Christian meditation is based on three very important truths. The first is that the risen Lord Jesus is mysteriously present with His disciples as He promised in Matthew 28:20: "I am with you always, to the end of the age." This truth, that is, Christ's presence, makes Christian meditation different from other techniques that either relive past events or visualize a desirable scenario. When we meditate on Jesus, we aren't playing mind games; we don't fantasize and imagine unrealities. We envisage what we know to be true. We interact with Christ, who is actually present with us invisibly. He would indeed be visible and audible to us if we but had eyes to see and ears to hear. Thus, when we meditate on a story from the Gospels, the risen Lord Jesus ministers to us just as He ministered to people when He was visibly and palpably present two thousand years ago.

The second truth is that Christ's Word has life-giving power because it is inspired by the Holy Spirit (John 6:63). This truth is the foundation for the teaching and practice of meditation in the Church. Unlike human words, which accomplish comparatively little or nothing, Christ's Word is powerful and effective. It does what it says. So, when Jesus speaks of healing and forgiveness, He actually heals and forgives people through His Word. He speaks with authority and power. His words are active and performative because they are inspired by and filled with the Holy Spirit. Through His Word Jesus gives His Holy Spirit and grants eternal life to those who trust in Him. His Spirit and His Word belong together and work together. Through faithful meditation on Christ's Word we receive the Holy Spirit and experience the power of the Spirit in our lives.

The third truth is that God the Father has justified us by His grace through our faith in Christ and His Word. Luther explores the connection between justification by grace and meditation in his commentary on Psalm 1. He notes that "delight" in God's Word leads to meditation on it. The problem is that those who lack the assurance of salvation fear and despise His Word because it reveals their guilt and makes them try to justify themselves before God. Their uneasy conscience distorts their hearing of His Word and so prevents them from receiving His good gifts. Since they take no delight in God's Word, they have little or no interest in it. The righteous, those who are sure of God's approval and depend on Christ for their salvation, delight in God's Word because it justifies them and brings the blessings of God to them as a free gift. For them, meditation is a joyful exercise of their faith in Christ; through it they receive the gifts of God and have Him do His work in them. So faith in Christ provides the foundation for fruitful meditation on God's Word. By faith, meditation becomes an experience of God's grace rather than just another futile attempt at self-justification and spiritual self-advancement.

When we meditate, we fix our attention on Jesus and His Word. Through meditation on that Word we receive grace upon grace from Christ (John 1:16). Through faith we stand with Jesus in the Father's presence and behold the hidden glory of the Word made flesh (1:14; 17:24). That spiritual perception comes through hearing God's Word and meditating on it. Our meditation depends on God and His presence with us.

Faithful Meditation

When I meditate, the thing on which I meditate and my attitude to it largely determines what happens to me as I meditate. Take, for example, the memory of a happy event, like the day I got married. As I replay it in my imagination, I enjoy it once again. As I relive that day, it occupies my mind and makes me feel good about it and my marriage once again. How different it would be if I were unhappily married! The same applies to any memory. The better the event, the more positive the effect of meditation on it; the worse the event, the more negative the effect of meditation on it.

When we meditate on Christ and His Word, the power of His Word and our attitude to it determines what happens to us as we meditate.

Christ's Word differs from our words because He is God's Son; His Word is both human and divine. When I speak, my words have a limited impact on people because I am just a human being. But when Christ speaks, things happen. His words are powerful and effective. They do what He says; they give what He offers. So when I tell sick people to get well, my words may provide some comfort, but they do not actually make them well. But when Jesus speaks the same words, the sick are actually healed. They get well because when He speaks, His Spirit, the Holy Spirit, is given to those who believe that He does exactly what He says.

Christian meditation differs from all other kinds of meditation because it concentrates on what Jesus says; it is meditation on His Word as it is given to us in the Scriptures. We meditate on His powerful Word. His Word has an impact on us as we pay attention to it, does its work in us as we listen to it, and reshapes us inwardly as we let it have its say. The words of Jesus actually produce our meditation. Yet that does not happen automatically but only as we put our trust in it.

As Christians, we have all experienced the power of God's Word in us as a word of judgment and salvation. Its impact on our conscience is described most vividly in Hebrews 4:12–13:

> For the word of God is living and active, sharper than any two-edged sword, piercing to the division of soul and of spirit, of joints and of marrow, and discerning the thoughts and intentions of the heart. And no creature is hidden from His sight, but all are naked and exposed to the eyes of Him to whom we must give account.

As we meditate on God's Word, we stand spiritually naked before God and in His sight. His Word puts us face-to-face with Him. That Word penetrates and exposes the secret reaches of our hearts; it lays us bare before God and holds us accountable to Him. But, best of all, it does all this so that it can give us life and do its work in us.

Martin Luther explains the power of meditation on God's Word most memorably in a sermon that he preached on Christmas Day in 1519. There he speaks about "sacramental" meditation on the Gospels and their stories about Jesus:

> All the words and stories of the gospels are sacraments of a kind, sacred signs by which God works in believers what the histories signify. Just as baptism is the sacrament by which God restores us;

just as absolution is the sacrament by which God forgives sins, so the words of Christ are sacraments through which he works salvation. Hence the gospel is to be taken sacramentally, that is, the words of Christ need to be meditated on as symbols through which that righteousness, power, and salvation is given which these words themselves portray. . . . We meditate properly on the gospel when we do so sacramentally, for through faith the words produce what they portray. Christ was born; believe that he was born for you and you will be born again. Christ conquered death and sin; believe that he conquered them for you and you will conquer them. (WA 9:439, 442; Kleinig's translation)

When Luther speaks of the words of Christ as sacraments, he is not using the term in its narrow sense, but more broadly as a divine enactment, a sacred sign that conveys what it signifies. Neither God's Word by itself nor faith in itself produces the kind of meditation that God desires. Rather, meditation is the exercise of faith in Christ and His performative Word, for faith receives what Christ gives to us through His Word. We receive, as we believe.

We can best see how this kind of sacramental meditation works from Luther's instruction on how to read a story in the Gospels. He gives this helpful advice in his 1521 pamphlet "A Brief Instruction on What to Look for and Expect in the Gospels":

When you open the book containing the gospels and read or hear how Christ comes here or there, or how someone is brought to him, you should therein perceive the sermon or the gospel through which he is coming to you, or you are being brought to him. For the preaching of the gospel is nothing else than Christ coming to us, or we being brought to him. When you see how he works, however, and how he helps everyone to whom he comes or who is brought to him, then rest assured that faith is accomplishing this in you and that he is offering your soul exactly the same sort of help and favor through the gospel. If you pause here and let him do you good, that is, if you believe that he benefits and helps you, then you really have it. Then Christ is yours, presented to you as a gift. (AE 35:121)

Here Luther gives a new twist to an ancient Christian method of meditation that looked at the text of a story in three stages. First, it used all the five senses to imagine the scenario of the event, vividly and concretely. Then, those who pondered on it applied the story to their situation by identifying themselves with the main character or characters in it. Finally, a story was used to work out how one might respond in obedience to Christ.

In the light of this ancient tradition, two things are remarkable about Luther's teaching on meditation. On the one hand, he teaches us to meditate on each story in the Gospels evangelically as the preaching of Good News rather than a demand for obedience. The story is to be heard, first and foremost, as the Good News of Christ's coming in person to those who meditate on it. It is Good News because through that story Christ comes to offer Himself and His gifts to those who hear it. This method, of course, would be nothing but an exercise in wishful thinking if it were not for the real presence of the risen Lord Jesus with us. But since He is now actively present with us, we may, quite rightly, identify ourselves with those who received help from Jesus. What He said and did then, He says and does to us here and now. Each story about Jesus, which itself was shaped by the meditation of the apostles on what Jesus said and did in His earthly ministry, is meant to be an aid for meditation.

On the other hand, Luther encourages us to meditate on the story faithfully. He assumes that each story is meant to inspire us to trust in Jesus and to turn to Him for help. Through the story of His interaction with people long ago, Christ comes and produces faith in us who hear about His words and deeds. As we put our trust in Him, we receive the same help and favor that He gave to the people who, back then, came to Him or were brought to Him. As we believe that the same Lord Jesus is now saying or doing the same good thing to us, we experience His hidden intervention in our lives here and now. By faithful meditation on His Word, we receive Christ as a gift. Thus meditation becomes, basically, a matter of reception from Him rather than an act of obedience to Him.

—From *Grace Upon Grace: Spirituality for Today*
(St. Louis: Concordia, 2008), pp. 95–98, 99–104.

APPENDICES

Mining More Treasures of Truth

You've come to the end of this book, but you are nowhere near the end of the journey that is your life in Christ. There is always more to rejoice in, always more to know, always more to marvel and wonder at when you continue to study prayerfully God's Word and meditate on the majesty and mystery of the truth about Jesus Christ. Spend some time with the chronology of Jesus Christ's life and read around in the various accounts provided in the Gospel. It's like studying a brilliant diamond—you are always going to see some new aspect of its beauty as it turns and sparkles, so also and even more when you reflect on Jesus.

Catalog of Testimonies

Strong Stuff to Use When People Have More Questions about the Lutheran Confession of the Two Natures in Christ

What Is This?

The *Catalog of Testimonies* was appended to several early editions of the Book of Concord to show that Lutheran teaching about the two natures in Christ is thoroughly in line with the historic and universal faith of the Christian Church. The doctrine of the two natures in Christ, known as Christology, is the foundation for the Bible's teaching about justification. Justification without biblical Christology becomes a philosophical abstraction. Christology makes justification what it is: a powerful, present, joyful reality through Word and Sacrament by means of which the God-man, Jesus Christ, is present with us, and for us, according to both His divine and human natures, giving us forgiveness, life, and salvation. Reformed theologians denied that Christ's human nature is present under the bread and wine of the Lord's Supper and accused Lutherans of making up new understandings about the two natures in Christ. Therefore, it was necessary for Lutherans to refute these claims and show that their doctrine is, in fact, thoroughly in keeping with Scripture and the Ancient Church Fathers, who taught the same things. The translation is based on the Latin text.

In these quotations, the divine nature of Christ is often referred to as "the Word," a reference to John 1, in which the Son of God is referred to as "the Word."

Abbreviations

References are given as to where the quotes may be found. Some of these (e.g., those to Migne) are in the original language. Where available, references are provided to English translations (e.g., *The Nicene and Post-Nicene Fathers of the Church*). Here is a key to the reference sources:

ANF = *Ante-Nicene Fathers*. Ed. Alexander Roberts and James Donaldson. Edinburgh: T&T Clark.

CSEL = *Corpus Scriptorum Ecclesiasticorum Latinorum*

Denzinger = *Enchiridion symbolorum definitionum et declarationum de rebus fidei et morum*. Ed. Heinrich Denzinger and Peter Huennermann. Freiburg: Herder, 1991.

Epistolae = *Epistolae Romanorum Pontificum Genuinae et quae ad eos Scriptae Sunt*. Ed. Andreas Thiel. Braunsberg: Peter, 1868.

Ferrar = *The Proof of the Gospel: Being the Demonstratio Evangelical of Eusebius of Caesarea*. Ed. W. J. Ferrar. New York: Macmillan, 1920.

Library = *Library of the Fathers of the Holy Catholic Church*. Trans. E. B. Pusey, et al. Oxford: Parker, 1836–85.

MPG = *Patrologiae cursus completus: Series Graece*. Ed. Jacques-Paul Migne. 161 vols. Paris and Turnhout, 1857–66.

MPL = *Patrologiae cursus completus: Series Latina*. Ed. Jacques-Paul Migne. 221 vols. Paris, 1844–80.

NPNF = *Nicene and Post-Nicene Fathers*. Ed. Philip Schaff. New York: Christian Literature Publishing, 1892.

Robinson = *Nag Hammadi and Manichaean Studies*. Ed. J. M. Robinson and H. J. Klimkeit. Leiden: Brill, 1994.

Theophylact = *The Explanation by Blessed Theophylact of the Holy Gospel according to St. Matthew*. House Springs, MO: Chrysostom Press, 1992.

Catalog of Testimonies

From Scripture and the orthodox Ancient Church that show what Scripture and the Early Church taught about the person of Christ and the Divine Majesty of His human nature, who is exalted to God's omnipotent right hand. They also show what forms of speech are used by Scripture and the orthodox Early Church.

To the Christian Reader

Some people claim that the Book of Concord deviates from the phrases and ways of speaking used by the pure, Ancient Church and Church Fathers, particularly in those articles concerning the person of Christ. They say that new, strange, made-up, unusual, and unheard-of expressions have been introduced. The Book of Concord appeals to the Ancient Church and Church Fathers, but many quotations from the Church Fathers were too long to include in the Book of Concord itself. Excerpts were carefully prepared and delivered to several electors and princes. They are printed here as an appendix at the end of the Book of Concord, in regard to particular points, for the purpose of providing the reader a thorough and correct accounting.

A person will easily recognize that when these doctrines are taught in the Book of Concord nothing new has been introduced, either in the doctrinal issues themselves, or in phrases and ways of speaking. We have spoken and taught about these mysteries, first of all, just as Holy Scripture does, and also as the ancient, pure Church did. Therefore, when the Book of Concord teaches about the unity of the person of Christ, the distinction of the two natures in Christ, and their essential properties, it is doing so just as the Fathers and councils of the ancient, pure Church have. They all taught that there are not two persons, but one Christ. In this person there are two distinct natures, the divine and the human, which are not separated or intermingled or transformed into each other. Each nature has and retains its essential attributes, to all eternity, never laying them aside. The essential attributes of the one nature, which are truly and properly ascribed to the entire Person, never become attributes of the other nature. This is proven by the following testimonies from the ancient pure councils.

The Council of Ephesus

Canon 4:

> If anyone divides the words of Scripture that speak about the two persons, or hypostases, of Christ and apply some of them to Him as a man in such a way that the Word is separated from God, or without the Word of the Father, or takes other statements from Scripture and says they apply only to Him as God, that is the Word from God the Father, let him be accursed.

Canon 5:

> If anyone dares to say that the man *Christ* is the Bearer of God, and instead of saying that He is God, truly the Son of God by nature, the "Word made flesh," who was made a partaker of flesh and blood precisely like us, let him be accursed.

Canon 6:

> If anyone does not confess that Christ is, at the same time, God and man, because, according to the Scriptures, the Word was made flesh, let him be accursed.

Canon 12:

> If anyone does not confess that the Word of God suffered in the flesh, was crucified in the flesh, and tasted death in the flesh, becoming the firstborn from the dead, although as God He is life and gives life, let him be accursed. (Denzinger, 255–57, 263)

The Council of Chalcedon (AD 451)

As cited by Evagrius, book 2, chapter 4:

> Following the holy Fathers, we confess one and the same Son, our Lord Jesus Christ. With one voice we confess that He is perfect in deity and perfect in humanity. He is truly God and truly man, consisting of a rational soul and body. He is consubstantial with the Father in regard to His deity and is consubstantial with us according to His humanity. He is like us in every way, except He is without sin. He was begotten before the world out of the Father according to His divinity. The same person was, in the last days, born for us and for our salvation from the Virgin Mary, the Mother of God, according to His humanity. We confess that one and the same Jesus Christ, the Son, the Lord, the only-begotten, is known in two natures, without

commingling, without changing, without division and without separation. The difference between the two natures is in no way abolished because of the Personal Union. The unique aspects of each nature are preserved. They are not run together into one person and substance, neither divided or torn into two persons. There is one and the same only-begotten Son, God the Word and the Lord Jesus Christ. ‹We acknowledge one single Lord Christ who is at one and the same time the only-begotten Son, the Word of the Father and also true man.› The prophets of old and the Christ Himself have taught us these things concerning Him, as well as the symbol that the Fathers have handed down to us. (*MPG*, 86:2507/8C–2509/10A)

Tenth Synodical Letter of Leo to Flavianus ‹Used by the Council of Chalcedon›

Tenth Synodical Epistle of Leo to Flavianus (chapter 3, folio 92):

‹The Personal Union has taken place in this way.› The distinct aspects of each nature are unimpaired. ‹The two natures remain unmingled and unchanged.› Each nature comes together into one person. Therefore, Divine Majesty assumes human lowliness. Divine Power assumes human weakness. ‹The Eternal Divine Being assumes the› mortality of human nature (abstract for the concrete). For the purpose of paying the debt of our condition, the immortal nature that cannot suffer has been united to the human nature that can suffer. This happened so that the same Mediator could die according to one nature, and could not die according to the other nature ‹in order that our single Mediator, who could not die according to the Divine Nature, might die for us according to the human nature›.

Likewise (chapter 4, folio 93):

He who is truly God is also truly man, since both the humility of the man and the loftiness of God ‹exist in one person›. Just as God did not change when He took pity ‹on us and assumed the human nature›, so man was not consumed by divine dignity ‹and glory›. For each nature does what is unique to it, in communion with the other. The Word does what belongs to the Word, ‹the Son of God,› and the flesh carries out what belongs to the flesh. One of these natures flashes forth in the miracles, the other sinks beneath injuries. ‹Yes, there is still one single Mediator, God and man.› He is God because in the beginning was the Word and the Word was God, by whom all things were made. He is man because the Word was made flesh, and because He was born of woman. We read that the Son of Man descended from heaven when the Son of God assumed flesh of the Virgin Mary, thus indicating the unity of the Person with two natures.

And again (chapter 5, folio 93):

It is said that the Son of God was crucified and buried. He suffered these things not in His very divinity, by which He is consubstantial with the Father, but in the infirmity of ‹His assumed› human nature. [Denzinger, 293–95]

So far the words of the Council of Ephesus and of Chalcedon. These councils agree with all the other holy Fathers.

This is precisely what the learned men in our schools want to indicate when they speak of these matters in the abstract and the concrete. ‹The Book of Concord› refers to this fact when it says of these issues, "All of which the learned know well." These words must be retained in their true sense in the schools.

Concrete terms are words that refer to the entire person in Christ, such as *God* and *man*. Abstract terms are words used to talk about the two natures in Christ, such as *divinity* and *humanity*.

Therefore, according to this distinction, it is correct to say, speaking concretely [*in concreto*], "God is man and man is God." On the other hand it is incorrect to say, speaking abstractly [*in abstracto*], "Divinity is humanity and humanity is divinity."

The same rule applies also to the essential attributes of each nature in Christ. This means that the attributes of one nature cannot be predicated of the other nature in the abstract, as though they were attributes of the other nature. Therefore, the following expressions would be false and incorrect. It would be wrong for a person to say, "The human nature is Omnipotence and is from eternity." Thus, again, since the attributes of one nature in Christ cannot be predicated of the other, one could not say, "Mortality is immortality and immortality is mortality." If one were to speak this way, the distinction between the two natures in Christ and their attributes would be abolished. They would be confounded with each other, changed into the other, and thus made equal and alike.

We must not only know, but also firmly believe, that the human nature that Christ received into His person has, and retains to all eternity, its essence and the naturally essential attributes. This is very important and the greatest consolation for Christians. We must also know from the revelation of Holy Scripture, and not doubt, the majesty to which the human nature has truly and actually been elevated by the Personal Union. The human nature has become a personal participant in the divine majesty.

These truths have been extensively explained in the Book of Concord, which has not introduced new, strange, made-up, unheard-of paradoxes and expressions into the Church of God. To show this to everyone, the following Catalog of Testimonies, first from the Holy Scriptures, then also from the ancient, pure teachers of the Church, especially from leaders in the first four ecumenical councils, will show how they have spoken about the person of Christ and the two natures in Christ. These quotations have been arranged under several distinct topics, so that the Christian reader will find it easier to work his way through them.

I.

The majesty of the divine nature is communicated to the human nature. When the Holy Scriptures, and also the Fathers, speak of the majesty that the human nature of Christ has received through the personal union, they use the words *communication, communion, sharing, bestowed,* and *given.*

> Behold, with the clouds of heaven there came one like a son of man, and He came to the Ancient of Days and was presented before Him. And to Him was given dominion and glory and a kingdom, that all peoples, nations, and languages should serve Him; His dominion is an everlasting dominion, which shall not pass away, and His kingdom one that shall not be destroyed. (Daniel 7:13–14)

> Jesus, knowing that the Father had given all things into His hands. (John 13:3)

> All things have been handed over to Me by My Father. (Matthew 11:27)

> All authority in heaven and on earth has been given to Me. (Matthew 28:18)

> Therefore God has highly exalted Him and bestowed on Him the name that is above every name, so that at the name of Jesus every knee should bow, in heaven and on earth and under the earth. (Philippians 2:9–10)

> And He put all things under His feet. (Ephesians 1:22; [see also Psalm 8:6;] 1 Corinthians 15:27; Hebrews 2:8)

Eusebius, Evangelical *Demonstration*, book 4, chapter 13:

> The Word of the Father has of Himself *communicated* what was His to the received man. He has communicated divine power to the received mortal nature, but has not received for Himself anything out of the mortal nature. (*MPG*, 22:288A/B; Ferrar, 1:188)

And again, chapter 14:

> The Word, making this human being worthy of eternal life as he has always been, and putting him in communion in His deity and blessedness. (*MPG*, 22:289A; Ferrar, 1:190–91)

Athanasius, *Letter to Epictetus*, quoted also by Epiphanius against the Dimoeritae (*Heresies*, 77):

> The Word did not become flesh in order to add to divinity. In order that flesh might rise up, He came forth from Mary, not that the Word might become better. There was a great addition to the human body from communion and union with the Word. (*MPG*, 42:656C, 26:1065A/B; *NPNF*, ser. 2, 4:573)

Epiphanius, *Heresies*, 69:

> It is clear that the flesh from Mary and that came from our race was transformed into glory in the Transfiguration, having acquired the glory of the Godhead, heavenly honor and perfection and glory which the flesh did not have from the beginning, but received in the union with God the Word. (*MPG*, 42:332D; Robinson, 26: *The Panarion of Epiphanius of Salamis, Books 2 and 3*, 398–99)

Cyril, *Dialogue*, book 5:

> How, then, does the flesh of Christ make alive? He replies: Because of the union with the living Word, which is accustomed to communicate the endowments of His nature to His own body. (*MPG*, 75:962B–963C)

Theodoret, *Interpretation of the Epistle to the Ephesians*:

> That the nature received from us is a *participant* in the same honor of Him who received it and that no difference in worship appears, but the divinity which is not seen is worshiped through the nature which is seen— this surpasses every miracle. (*MPG*, 82:517A)

Damascene, in Book 3, *Of the Orthodox Faith*, chapters 7, 15:

> ‹The Divine Nature *communicates* or› *imparts* its own excellent qualities to the flesh, while remaining incapable of suffering. It does not share in the sufferings of the flesh. (*MPG*, 94:1012C, 1058C; *NPNF*, ser. 2, 9[pt. 2]:52)

Also, in chapter 19:

> The flesh has communion with the divine operations of the Word, because the divine operations are carried out through the body. He that

works both in a divine and human fashion is one. It is necessary to know that just as His holy mind carries out natural human functions, so also it participates in the divinity of the Word. The Word works, arranges, governs, perceives, knows and determines everything, not simply as the mind of a man, but as being made one in person with God, as being constituted with the mind of God. (*MPG*, 94:1080B/C; *NPNF*, ser. 2, 9[pt. 2]:68)

II.

Christ received divine majesty here in time, not according to His divine nature, but according to the human nature that He received, that is, according to the flesh, as man, or the Son of Man.

‹Testimony from the Holy Scriptures:›

After making purification for sins, He sat down at the right hand of the Majesty on high. (Hebrews 1:3)

At present, we do not yet see everything in subjection to Him. But we see Him who for a little while was made lower than the angels, namely Jesus, crowned with glory and honor because of the suffering of death. (Hebrews 2:8–9)

But from now on the Son of Man shall be seated at the right hand of the power of God. (Luke 22:69)

And the Lord God will give to Him the throne of His father David, and He will reign over the house of Jacob forever, and of His kingdom there will be no end. (Luke 1:32–33)

He has granted the Son also to have life in Himself. And He has given Him authority to execute judgment, because He is the Son of Man. (John 5:26–27)

Testimonies from the Church Fathers:

Athanasius, quoted by Theodoret, Dialogue 2, page 330:

Whenever Scripture says that the Word received glory in time, it is speaking about His humanity, not His divinity. (*MPG*, 83:181A)

Athanasius, in the *Oration against the Arians*, 2 and 4 (f. 347. 490 f. 492, ed. Colon., 1686):

Scripture does not mean that the substance of the Word has been exalted. It is talking about His humanity. He is said to be exalted according to the flesh. Since it is His body, it is proper to say that as man He was exalted and received something, with respect to His body, according to His humanity. His body receives those things that the Word always possessed according to His deity and perfection from the Father. As a man, He says that He received the power that as God He always has. He who glorifies others, says, "Glorify me," in order to show that He had flesh that lacked such things. When the flesh of His humanity receives glorification, He speaks as if He Himself had received it.

Therefore we must always keep in mind when reading the Holy Scriptures that none of those things that He says He received in time, He received as though He did not already have them. For, being God and the Word, naturally He always had those things. But He says that He received them according to His humanity so that, even as He received them in Himself, in the flesh, He might in the future hand them over to us, from the same flesh, to be firmly possessed. (*MPG*, 26:95C, 98–99, 406B/C, 410A/B; *NPNF*, ser. 2, 4:330, 415)

Athanasius, *On the Assumed Humanity*, against Apollinarius (pp. 603 and 611, ed. Colon., 1686):

When Peter says that Jesus was God, both Lord and Christ, He is not talking about His divinity, but about His humanity. The Word was always Lord. He did not become Lord only after the cross. Rather, His divinity made the humanity both Lord and Christ. (*MPG*, 26:1022A/B)

And:

Whatever the Scriptures say that the Son has received, this is said in respect to receiving in His body. This body is the firstfruits of the Church. Accordingly, God raised up and exalted first His own body, but afterward members of His body. (*MPG*, 26:1003B)

With these words Athanasius explained what the whole Church said later.

Basil the Great, *Against Eunomius*, book 4 (p. 769, ed. Paris):

When the Lord is celebrated, and receives a name (Philippians 2:9) that is above every name, and when He says, "All authority in heaven and on earth has been given to Me" (Matthew 28:18) and "I live because of the Father" (John 6:57) and "Glorify Me … with the glory that I had with You before the world existed" (John 17:5) these things must be understood of the incarnation, not of His Deity. (*MPG*, 29:694C, 597C, 701A/B)

Ambrose:

You have learned that He can subject all things to Himself according to the operation of Deity. Learn now that He receives, according to His flesh, all things in subjection to Him, as it is written in Ephesians 1. According to the flesh, therefore, all things are delivered to Him as His subjects. (*MPL*, 19:714B; *NPNF* ser. 2, 10:307; *MPL*, numbers this chapter "15")

Ambrose, book 5, chapter 2 (p. 99):

God does give the apostles a participation in His seat, but to Christ, according to His humanity, He gives a common participation in the divine seat. (*MPL*, 16:691B; *NPNF*, ser. 2, 10:294)

And in chapter 6 (p. 108):

In Christ our common human nature has, according to the flesh, obtained the prerogative of the heavenly seat. (*MPL*, 16:713B; *NPNF*, ser. 1, 14:307; *MPL* numbers this chapter "4")

Chrysostom, Heb. 1, Serm. 3, p. 117 (tom. 4: *Homilies*, 3, p. 1493):

In regard to the flesh ‹the Father has commanded›, "Let all God's angels worship Him." (*MPG*, 63:28; *NPNF*, ser. 1, 14:375)

Theophylact, on John 3 (p. 235; ed. Paris, 1631, f. 605):

He gave all things into His Son's hand, according to humanity. (*MPG*, 123:1225A)

Oecumenius from Chrysostom, Heb. 1 (t. 2, op. p. 324, ed. 1631):

"As the Son of God, He has an eternal throne. 'Thy throne,' says God, 'is forever and ever.' After the cross and passion He was deemed worthy of honor, not as God, but as man, and He received what He had as God." And a little after: "Therefore, as man, He hears, 'Sit at My Right hand,' for as God He has eternal power." (*MPG*, 119:289A/B.)

Cyril, book 9, *Thesauri*, chapter 3 (tom. 2, p. 110):

As man, He ascended to ruling power. (*MPG*, 75:363C)

The same, book 2, chapter 17:

As man He sought glory that He always had as God. He doesn't say these things as though He had ever been destitute of His own glory, but because He wanted to bring His own temple [His body] into the glory that He always has as God. (*MPG*, 75:439/40A, a passage that expresses the idea of this citation, though not in its precise words)

The same, book 2, *Ad Reginas*:

That He received glory, power, and rule over all things must be referred to the conditions [properties] of *humanity*. (*MPG*, 76:1359C, a passage that expresses the idea of this citation, though not in its precise words)

Theodoret, on Psalm 2 (t. 1, p. 242):

Though Christ, as God, is by nature Lord, He receives universal power also as a man. (*MPG*, 80:880A)

On Psalm 110 (t. 1, p. 242):

"Sit at My right hand"—this was said *according to the human nature*. As God, He has eternal dominion. *As man*, He has received what He had as God. *As man*, therefore, He hears ‹what is said to Him›, "Sit at My right hand." For as God, He has eternal dominion. (*MPG*, 80:1768B)

On Hebrews 1 (t. 2, p. 154) Theodoret says:

Christ always received worship and adoration from the angels, for He always was God. Now they are adoring Him also as man. (*MPG*, 82:686C)

Leo, Epist. 23 (folio 99; Ep. [23 and 83] 46 and 97, ff. 261 and 317, ed. Lugd., 1700), treating of Eph. 1, says:

Let the enemies of the truth openly explain when, and according to which nature, the almighty Father raised His Son above all things, and similarly, according to what nature He subjected all things. All things have always been subject to His divine nature, as Creator. If power was added to the divine nature, or His sublime divine nature was exalted, then that means it was inferior to Him who did the exalting. It would mean that the divine nature of Christ actually was in need of something to be added to it and that it depended on another divine nature. Arius welcomes those who hold such views into his fellowship. (*MPL*, 54:869; *NPNF*, ser. 2, 12:59)

Leo, Epist. 83 (folio 134):

We understand that "exaltation" and "a name above every name" have to do with the human nature, which was enriched by a great increase in glorification, although there is absolutely one and the same person, divine and human. In the incarnation nothing was taken away from the Word that had to be returned to it by means of a gift from the Father. The "form of a servant" is the human nature's humility, which now has been exalted to the glory of divine power. So, divine things were never done without man, human things [never] done without God. (*MPL*, 54:1066; *NPNF*, ser. 2, 12:94)

Whatever Christ has received in time He has received as man. Things are conferred on man, which he did not have; however, according to the Word, the Son also has all things, in no way different from what the Father has. (*MPL*, 54:1066–67; *NPNF*, ser. 2, 12:94)

Vigilius, book 5, *Against Eutyches* (Ep. 66 sq., ed. Divion., 1664. 4):

The divine nature does not need to be elevated to honor, or to be increased by advancing its dignity. The divine nature does not need to merit all power on heaven and earth through obedience. Therefore, according to the fleshly nature, He [Christ] acquired these things. According to the nature of the Word he never lacked them. Did the Creator have to obtain these things as a gift in these last times because He had no power and dominion over his creature? (*MPL*, 62:141A/D, 142B)

Nicephorus, book 1, chapter 36 (folio 86):

His disciples saw Him on the mount of Transfiguration, where He affirmed that the highest power in heaven and earth had been given to Him, according to His humanity. (*MPG*, 145:742B)

III.

The Holy Scriptures, likewise the holy Fathers of the ancient, pure Church, speak about this mystery in abstract terms, making it very clear that the human nature, by means of the personal union, truly and actually receives and uses the majesty of the divine nature.

Whoever feeds on My flesh and drinks My blood has eternal life. . . . For My flesh is true food, and My blood is true drink. (John 6:54–55)

The blood of Jesus His Son cleanses us from all sin. (1 John 1:7)

How much more will the blood of Christ, who through the eternal Spirit offered Himself without blemish to God, purify our conscience from dead works to serve the living God. (Hebrews 9:14)

Take, eat; this is My body . . . Drink of it, all of you, for this is My blood of the covenant (Matthew 26:26–28)

Eustachius, quoted by Theodoret, Dialogue 2 (p. 40):

He prophesied that He ‹, that is, Christ the man, the human nature of Christ,› would sit on a holy throne and share it with the Divine Spirit, thus showing that God dwells in Him without separation. (*MPG*, 83:176B)

The same, quoted in Gelasius:

The man Christ, who increased in wisdom, age and favor, received dominion over all things. (*Epistolae*, 1:544)

And:

Christ, in His very body, came to His apostles and said, "All power in heaven and on earth has been given to me." It was the external temple that received this power, not God ‹, that is, not according to His divinity,› which built the external temple of extraordinary beauty. (*Epistolae*, 1:554)

Athanasius, *On the Arian and the Catholic Confession* (t. 2, op. p. 579, ed. Colon.):

God was not changed into human flesh or substance, but in Himself glorified the nature that He received, so that the human, weak, mortal flesh and nature received divine glory in order to have all power in heaven and on earth, which it did not have before it was received by the Word. (This work was traditionally assigned to Athanasius in the Middle Ages but was in fact composed by Vigilius of Thapsus; *MPL*, 62:305B)

The same author (*l.c.*, pp. 597 and 603), *On the Assumed Humanity*, against Apollinarius (p. 530):

In Philippians 2, Paul talks about His body as a temple. His flesh is exalted, not He who is the Most Exalted One. To His flesh He gave the name above every name, that at the name of Jesus every knee should bow and every tongue confess that Jesus Christ is the Lord, to the glory of the Father.

Athanasius adds a general rule:

When Scripture talks about the glorification of Christ, it is talking about the flesh, which has received glory. Whatever Scripture says that the Son has received, it is saying this according to His humanity, not His divinity. So, when the Apostles say that all the fullness of the Godhead dwells bodily in Christ, we must understand that this fullness dwells in the flesh of Christ. (*MPG*, 26:987–90)

The same author, quoted by Theodoret, Dialogue 2 (t. 3, p. 286):

"Sit on My right hand," has been said to the Lord's body.

Also:

Therefore, it is the body to which He says, "Sit on My right hand." (*MPG*, 83:180B)

Athanasius, *On the Incarnation*, as quoted in Cyril in his *Defense of the Eighth Anathema*, and in his book *On the True Faith to the Queens*:

The holy catholic Church condemns anyone who says that the human flesh of our Lord is not to be worshiped and adored as the flesh of the Lord and God. (*MPG*, 76:350C, 1211)

The same, *On Humanity Assumed* (p. 603, ed. Colon.):

Whatever Scripture says that the Son has received, it understands as having been received *according to His body*. His body is the firstfruits of the Church; therefore, the Lord first raised and exalted His body, and afterward also the members of His body. (*MPG*, 26:1003B)

Hilary, book 9 (p. 136):

Since the Word received human flesh, the flesh was united to the glory of the Word and possesses the glory of the Word. Thus, the man Jesus remained in the glory of God the Father. (*MPL*, 10:326–27; *NPNF*, ser. 2, 9:167)

Eusebius of Emissa, in his homily on the Sixth Holiday after Easter (*Feria 6, paschatos in homiliis, patrum*, p. 297):

He who, according to His divinity, always had power over all things with the Father and the Holy Spirit, now also according to His humanity has received power over all things. This man who suffered not long ago rules over heaven and earth and in fact does here and there whatever He wants to do. (*MPG*, 86:486–88)

Gregory of Nyssa, quoted by Gelasius and Theodoret, Dialogue 2 (t. 2, p. 333):

Acts 2:33 says that Christ was exalted to the right hand of God. Who was exalted? The lowly one or the highest one? What is lowly, except the human nature? Who else besides the divine is the highest? God, being the Highest, does not need to be exalted. The apostle says that the human nature was exalted by becoming Lord and Christ. Therefore, when the apostle says that God exalted Him, this does not mean that the Lord was, before the world, existing in some lower estate. What it means is that what was lowly, His human nature, was exalted to the right hand of God. . . . The right hand of God the Creator, the Lord, the one by whom all things were made and without whom nothing that exists was made, has itself, through the union, raised up to its own height the man who was united with it. (*MPG*, 83:193, 195; see also *Epistolae*, 1:549)

Basil the Great, *Against Eunomius*, book 2 (p. 661, ed. Paris):

⟨In Acts 2, when Peter says,⟩ "God has made the same Jesus whom you crucified both Lord and Christ," he is using the words ⟨"the same"⟩ to refer almost entirely to the human nature, seen by all. . . . When he says, "God has made Him both Lord and Christ," he is saying that power and dominion over all things was entrusted ⟨to His humanity⟩ by the Father. (*MPG*, 29:577A/B)

Epiphanius, *Against the Ariomanites* (p. 327, t. 1; folio 728, ed. Paris, 1638):

⟨When Peter adds,⟩ "this same Jesus whom you crucified" ⟨it is obvious that he is talking about the *incarnation* of the Lord, that is, His flesh,⟩ so that the incarnate flesh might not be left behind by the uncreated Word that cannot suffer, but might be united above to the uncreated Word. This is why God made that which was conceived by Mary and united to deity, both Lord and Christ. (*MPG*, 42:268B/C; Robinson, 360)

Ambrose, book 3, chapter 12, *Of the Holy Ghost* (t. 2, p. 157 [folio 765, ed. Colon.]):

Angels do not adore only the divinity of Christ, but also His footstool. . . . The prophet says that the earth the Lord took upon Himself when He assumed flesh is to be adored. Therefore, we understand "footstool" to mean the earth, that is, the flesh of Christ, which we today also adore in the Sacraments, and which the apostles adored in the Lord Jesus. (*MPL*, 16:827A, 828B–829A; *NPNF*, ser. 2, 10:145–46; *MPL* numbers this chapter "11")

Augustine, *Of the Words of the Lord*, Discourse 58 (t. 10, p. 217):

If Christ is not, by nature, God, but a creature, He is not to be worshiped or adored as God. They may reply and say, "But why do you adore His flesh if you admit that it is a creature? Why are you as devoted to His flesh as you are to His divinity?" (*MPL*, 39:2200)

Augustine answers:

It says, "Worship His footstool" (Psalm 99:5). His footstool is the earth. Christ took upon Himself earth of earth, because flesh is of the earth. He received His flesh from the flesh of Mary. Because He walked here in this same flesh, He gave us this very flesh to eat for salvation. No one who eats this flesh does not first worship it. Therefore, this is why the footstool of the Lord is worshiped. We not only not sin by worshiping it, we sin if we do not worship it. (*MPL*, 37:1264; *NPNF*, ser. 1, 8:485)

Chrysostom, on Hebrews 2 (p. 125):

It is great and wonderful and awe-inspiring that our flesh is seated above and worshiped by angels and archangels, by seraphim and cherubim. When I reflect on this, I am entranced ‹and seem to be outside of myself›. (*MPG*, 63:47; *NPNF*, ser. 1, 14:388)

The same, on 1 Corinthians 10 (p. 174, t. 6, p. 740, and t. 5, p. 261, ed. Frankf.):

This body, even when it is lying in a manger, is worshiped by the Magi. They took a long trip, and when they arrived, they worshiped with a lot of fear and trembling. (*MPG*, 61:202; *NPNF*, ser. 1, 12:143)

The same, in Epist. 65 to Leo:

Let us learn to know to which nature the Father said, "Share My seat." It is the same nature to which had been said, "You are dust and to dust you shall return."

Theophylact, from Chrysostom, on Matthew 28 (p. 311 [ed. Lutet., 8, 1631, fols. 184. 605]):

Since the human nature, which is united with the Word and only shortly before been condemned, is now seated in heaven, it is appropriate for Him to have said, "All power is given to Me in heaven." For the human nature, only recently having served, is now, in Christ, ruling over all things. (*MPG*, 123:484D; *Theophylact*, 257–58)

The same, on John 3:

He has given all things into the Son's hand, according to His humanity. (*MPG*, 123:1225A)

Cyril, *On the Incarnation*, chapter 11 (t. 4, p. 241; t. 5, p. 695):

> The Word introduced Himself into that which He was not, in order that man's nature might also become what it was not, being made resplendent with the grandeur of divine majesty, raised beyond nature, not that it has put the unchanging God beneath its nature. (*MPG*, 75:1383A; *Library*, 44:198)

Council of Ephesus (Cyril, t. 4, p. 140 [*Apologet, adv. Orient.*, t. 6, folio 196]), in Canon 11:

> If anyone does not confess that the flesh of the Lord makes alive, because it was made the Word's own flesh, who makes everything alive, let him be anathema. (*MPG*, 76:311)

Cyril also (*ibid.*, p. 140; t. 4, p. 85), in his explanation of this anathematization, says that Nestorius was unwilling to ascribe the ability to make alive to the *flesh* of Christ, but explained the passages in John 6 as referring to the divinity alone. (*MPG*, 76:311; *NPNF*, ser. 2, 14:217)

Theodoret, Dialogue 2:

> The body of the Lord was deemed worthy to be seated at the right hand of God. It is worshiped by every creature and is called the body of the Lord of Nature, ‹the body of God›. (*MPG*, 83:168C)

The same author, on Psalm 8:

> The human nature of Christ has received from God the honor of having dominion over the universe. (*MPG*, 80:920B)

Leo (folio 94 [Ep. 25, folio 246]), Epist. 11:

> It is a promotion of that which is received ‹, the human nature,› not of God, when it is said that God has exalted Him and has given Him a name above every name, the name of Jesus, at which every knee should bow, and every tongue confess that Jesus Christ is Lord to the glory of God the Father. (*MPL*, 54:807; *NPNF*, ser. 2, 12:49)

Damascene, book 3, chapter 18 (p. 251):

"Christ's divine will was eternal and omnipotent. His human will began in time and underwent its own natural and expected emotions. It was not omnipotent according to its own nature, but, because it truly and by nature became the will of God, it is also omnipotent." This means, as explained by a commentator: "The divine will has, by its own nature, the power to do all things that it wants to do, but Christ's human will does not have power to do everything it could do, by its nature, but it is united to God the Word." (*MPG*, 94:1076–77; *NPNF*, ser. 2, 9[pt. 2]:66)

The same, chapter 19:

> The flesh of Christ is in fellowship with the operating divinity of the Word. Divine actions are accomplished by means of the body because He who is working through the divinity and humanity is one. It is necessary to know that His holy mind works according to its natural functions and therefore shares in understanding, knowing, and managing all things ‹in the entire universe,› not as the mere mind of a man, but as personally united with God; it is the mind of God. (*MPG*, 94:1080B/C; *NPNF*, ser. 2, 9[pt. 2]:68)

The same, in the same book, chapter 21:

> The human nature does not, in and of itself, have knowledge of the future; but the Lord's soul, because of its personal identity and union with the Word Himself, apart from other divine criteria, was also rich in knowledge about the future. . . . We say that this Master and Lord of all creation, the one Christ, who is at the same time God and man, knows all things. For in Him are hidden all the treasures of wisdom and knowledge. (*MPG*, 94:1085A/C; *NPNF*, ser. 2, 9[pt. 2]:69)

Nicephorus, book 18, chapter 36:

> When Christ was seen by His disciples on the mount in Galilee, He asserted that the highest power in heaven and on earth has been given to Him by the Father, that is, according to His human nature. (*MPG*, 145:742B)

IV.

The Holy Scriptures, and the Fathers, understood that the majesty that Christ received in time included not only created gifts with their limited qualities, but also the glory and majesty of divinity that belongs to God, to which His human nature, in the person of the Son of God, had been exalted, and thus, the human nature received the power and efficacy of the divine nature that are peculiar to the Deity.

> And now, Father, glorify Me in Your own presence with the glory that I had with You before the world existed. (John 17:5)

> For in Him the whole fullness of deity dwells bodily. (Colossians 2:9)

Hilary, *On the Trinity*, book 3 (p. 28):

The Word made flesh prayed that that which was from time ‹, that is, has a beginning in time,› might receive the glory of that brightness, which is without time. (*MPL*, 10:85B; *NPNF*, ser. 2, 9[pt. I]:66)

Gregory of Nyssa, quoted by Gelasius and Theodoret, Dialogue 2, concerning the saying of Peter, Acts 2:

Being exalted by the right hand of God, etc. (t. 2, p. 333 [al. 330]): "This (right hand of God), through the union, raised to its own height the Man united to it. (*MPG*, 83:196; *Epistolae*, 1:549)

The same, *Concerning the Soul*:

God, the Word, is never changed by the communion that He has with the body and soul, neither does He partake of their imperfection; rather, He transmits to them the power of His divinity and remains the same that He was even before the union.

Basil the Great, *On the Holy Nativity of Christ* (p. 231):

How is Deity in the flesh? Just as fire is in iron, not by turning into iron, but by imparting itself into the iron. For fire does not run out to the iron, but remaining in its place, imparts its own specific power, which is not diminished when it is imparted. It fills the entire mass and becomes partaker of it. (Pseudo-Basil, *MPG*, 31:1460C)

Epiphanius, in Ancoratus (folio 504 [folio 86, ed. Colon.]):

Strengthening an earthly body with divinity, He united it into one power, brought it into one Divinity, being one Lord and one Christ, not two Christs nor two Gods, and so forth. (*MPG*, 43:168C/D)

Cyril, on John, book 4, chapter 23:

You are not entirely unwise when you deny that the flesh is able to make something alive. For if you are talking about the flesh alone, no, it cannot make anything alive at all. It is in need of something to make it alive. But when you are finished examining very carefully the mystery of the incarnation, having learned to know the life that dwells in the flesh, you will believe that although the flesh is not able to do anything by itself, it has nevertheless become life-giving, because it has been united to the life-giving Word. It has been joined to the Word and so now it has been made capable of giving life. The flesh of Christ did not drag the Word of God down to its corruptible nature; rather, the flesh was elevated to the power of the better nature. Therefore, although the nature of the flesh, insofar as it is flesh, cannot make anything alive; nevertheless, it is able to do this because it has received the entire operation of the Word. The flesh of Paul or Peter or others cannot do this, but that of Life itself in which the fullness of the Godhead dwells bodily, can do this. Therefore, the flesh of all others can do nothing, only the flesh of Christ can make alive, because in it dwells the only-begotten Son of God. (*MPG*, 73:602C; *Library*, 43:435)

Augustine, *Against Felicianus the Arian*, chapter 11:

I cannot agree that it is true to say that the Deity experienced the violence done to His body in the same way that we know the flesh was glorified by the majesty of the Deity. (*MPL*, 42:1165)

Theodoret, chapter *Of Antichrist* (t. 2, p. 411):

The Word that became man did not confer a partial grace on the received [human] nature; rather, it pleased God that the whole fullness of Deity dwelt in it. (*MPG*, 83:530–31)

The same, on Psalm 21 (t. 1, p. 110):

> If the received nature has been joined with the Divinity that received it, it participates and associates with the same glory and honor of the Divinity. (*MPG*, 80:1023C)

The same, on Hebrews 1:

> The human nature itself, after the resurrection, attained divine glory. (*MPG*, 82:683B)

Damascene, book 3, capp. 7. 15:

The divine nature imparts to the flesh its own excellences, while it remains impassible and does not participate in the passions of the flesh. (*MPG*, 94:1012C, 1058C; *NPNF*, ser. 2, 9[pt. 2]:52)

V.

Christ, as God, has divine majesty essentially in one way. It is His possession, part of His very essence, in and of Himself. As man He has it another way, as a result of the personal union, not in and of His very essence as a man.

I am the way, and the truth, and the life. (John 14:6)

He has granted the Son also to have life in Himself. . . . because He is the Son of Man. (John 5:26–27)

Cyril, book 12, *Thesauri*, chapter 15 (t. 2, p. 167 [t. 5, ed. Paris, 1638]):

There is one condition and quality pertaining to the creature and another to the Creator. Our nature, received by the Son of God, has exceeded its measure and by grace has been transferred into the condition of the One receiving it. (*MPG*, 75:535, 538)

The same, on John, book 2, chapter 144 (t. 1, p. 134 [t. 4, ed. Paris, 1638]):

Christ added the reason why He said that life and the power of judgment had been given Him by the Father. He said that it is because He is the Son of Man so that we would understand that all things were given to Him as man. However, the only-begotten Son is not a partaker of life, but is life by nature. (*MPG*, 73:383A/B; *Library*, 43:272)

The same, book 3, chapter 37 (t. 1, p. 181):

The body of Christ makes alive because it is the body of Life itself, retaining the power of the Word, now incarnate. It is full of the power of Him by whom all things exist and continue to live. (*MPG*, 73:519D–522A; *Library*, 43:376)

The same, book 4, chapter 14 (p. 201):

Because the Savior's flesh was joined to the Word of God, who is by nature Life, it was made life-giving. (*MPG*, 73:566D; *Library*, 43:410)

And chapter 18 (p. 204):

I filled My body with life. I received mortal flesh, but since I am by nature Life, I dwell in the flesh. I completely transformed it according to My life. (*MPG*, 73:586C; *Library*, 43:424)

Chapter 24 (p. 210):

The flesh, by its very nature, cannot on its own make anything alive. But in Christ it is not alone. It is united to the Son of God, who is in very essence Life. Therefore, when Christ says that His flesh gives life, He is not ascribing the power to make alive in the same way as He Himself, or His own Spirit, is able to make alive. For the Spirit makes alive by Himself. The flesh rises to this power by the personal union. We cannot understand with our minds or express with our tongue how this happens. We receive in silence and firm faith. (*MPG*, 73:603C/D; *Library*, 43:437)

The same, book 10, chapter 13 (p. 501):

The flesh of life, having been made the flesh of the Only-Begotten, has been brought to the power of life. (*MPG*, 74:343A/B)

The same, book 11, chapter 21 (p. 552):

Christ's flesh is not holy in and of itself. It is transformed by union with the Word into the power of the Word. It is the cause of salvation and sanctification to those who partake of it. Therefore, we say that that divinity works effectively through the flesh, not because of the flesh, but because of the Word. (*MPG* 74:519A)

Book 6, Dialogue (t. 5, op. ed. cit.):

Christ is glorified by the Father, not because He is God, but because He was man. It was not a result of His own nature that He was divinely effective. He received it by the union and ineffable concurrence that God the Word is understood to have with humanity. (*MPG*, 75:1026A)

From the same author, *On the True Faith, to Theodosius* (p. 278):

He introduced His life into the received human body by virtue of the union. (*MPG*, 76:1190A/B)

In the same place (p. 279):

The Word is life-giving because of the inexpressible birth from the living Father. Yet, we should recognize where the effectiveness of divine glory is ascribed also to His own flesh. Also: We confess that the earthly flesh is incapable of giving life, so far as its own nature is concerned. (*MPG*, 76:1190A/B)

Epiphanius, *Against the Ariomanites*, p. 337 (*Haeres.*, 69; p. 789, ed. Colon.):

His human nature was not something living apart, by itself; neither did He ever speak with the Divinity separated from the human nature, existing apart from it, as though they were two different persons, but always with the human nature united with the divine nature (there being one consecration), and even now the human nature knows the most perfect things because it is united in God and joined to the one Deity. (*MPG*, 42:305C/D; Robinson, 383)

Augustine, *Of the Words of the Lord*, Discourse 58 (t. 10, pp. 217–18):

I certainly do adore the Lord's flesh, yes, the perfect humanity in Christ, because it has been received by the divinity and united to Deity. I confess that there are not two different persons, but that one and same Son of God is God and man. In a word, if you separate man from God, I never believe or serve Him. (*MPL*, 39:220)

Also:

If anyone is disdainful about worshiping humanity, not a bare humanity by itself, but united to divinity, that is, the one Son of God, who is true God and true man, he will die eternally. (*MPL*, 39:220)

The same, *De Civitate*, book 10, chapter 24:

The flesh of Christ, by itself, does not cleanse believers, but through the Word, by which it has been received. (*MPL*, 41:301; *CSEL*, 40:486, 11; *NPNF*, ser. 1, 2:195)

Council of Ephesus, Canon 11 (in Cyril, t. 6, p. 196):

If anyone does not confess that the Lord's flesh is life-giving, for the reason that it was appropriated to the Word that gives life to all things, let him be anathema. (Denzinger, 262)

Theophylact, on John 3 (pp. 605, 184, ed. cit.):

He has given all things into His Son's hand, according to humanity. But if also according to divinity, what do we mean by this? The Father has given all things to the Son by reason of nature, not of grace. (*MPG*, 123:1225A)

The same, on Matthew 28:

If you want to understand the statement, "All power is given to Me in heaven and on earth," as something God said about the Word, then understand that this means that everyone, both the willing and unwilling, acknowledge Me as God. But when this is said of the human nature, then understand it this way: I, previously the condemned nature, am now truly God according to the unconfused union with the Son of God, and I have received power over all things. (*MPG*, 123:484–85; *Theophylact*, 258)

Damascene (book 3, chapter 17):

He did divine things not according to the capabilities of the flesh, but because the Word, united to His flesh, displayed its own capabilities. For glowing iron does not burn because of some natural power it has, but only because it is united with fire. Therefore, in itself the flesh is mortal, but because of its personal union to the Word, it is able to give life. (*MPG*, 94:1069B/C; *NPNF*, ser. 2, 9[pt. 2]:66)

The same author (chapter 18):

Christ's divine will was both eternal and omnipotent, etc. But His human will not only began in time, but also endured natural human qualities. It was not omnipotent, but because it truly has, by nature, become the will also of God the Word, it is also omnipotent. (*MPG*, 94:1076–77; *NPNF*, ser. 2, 9[pt. 2]:66)

This is, as explained by a commentator:

The divine will has, by its own nature, the power to do all things that it wants to do, but Christ's human will does not have power to do everything by nature, but only because it is united to God the Word.

The same author, in the same book, chapter 21:

The human nature does not possess essential knowledge of the future; but the soul of the Lord, because of its union with the Word and the personal identity with it, was rich in the knowledge of the future, in addition to other divine attributes. (And at the end of the chapter:) We say that the one Christ, Master, and Lord of all creation, at the same time God and man, knows also all things. For in Him are hid all the treasures of wisdom and knowledge. (*MPG*, 94:1085A/C; *NPNF*, ser. 2, 9[pt. 2]:69)

From the same author (Book 2, chapter 22):

Although the soul of the Lord by nature did not know the future, because it was personally united to the Word it had knowledge of all things, not by grace, but because of the personal union. (Shortly afterward:) Since the natures in our Lord Jesus Christ are distinct, the natural wills, that is, the powers of will, are also distinct. (*MPG*, 94:948A/B; *NPNF*, ser. 2, 9[pt 2]:69)

VI.

The divine nature powerfully demonstrates and actually exerts its majesty, power, and efficacy (which is unique to the divine nature and always remains so) in, with, and through the human nature that is personally united to it. The human nature has such majesty because the entire fullness of the Godhead dwells personally in the received human flesh and blood of Christ.

Whom God put forward as a propitiation by His blood. (Romans 3:25)

Since, therefore, we have now been justified by His blood. (Romans 5:9)

And through Him to reconcile to Himself all things, whether on earth or in heaven, making peace by the blood of His cross. (Colossians 1:20)

Athanasius, Oration 4, *Against the Arians* (*Epist. ad Adelph c. Arian*, t. 1, p. 161, ed. Colon.):

Why should the Lord's body not be worshiped when the Word, by stretching out His bodily hand, healed the person who was sick with a fever, and by speaking with a human voice raised Lazarus, and by extending His hands on the cross overthrew the prince of the air? (*MPG*, 26:1082B; *NPNF*, ser. 2, 4:577)

The same author, in Dialog 5, *Of the Trinity* (t. 2, op, f. 257):

God the Word, who was united to a man, does not perform miracles apart from the human nature. It has pleased him to work divine miracles through it, and in it, and with it. (And shortly afterward:) According to His good pleasure He made the humanity perfect above its own nature and did not prevent it from being a rational living being ‹, a creature, a true human nature›. (*MPG*, 28:1280–81)

Cyril, *De Recta Fide ad Theodosium* (t. 5, op.):

The soul, having obtained union with the Word, descended into hell; but, using its divine power and efficacy, it said to the ones in bondage, "Go forth!" (*MPG*, 76:1166A)

The same author, book 1, *Ad Reginas*:

Christ, as God, gives life through His own flesh. (*MPG*, 76:1282B)

VII.

The communication of divine majesty occurs also in glory, without mingling, annihilation, or denial of the human nature.

For the Son of Man is going to come with His angels in the glory of His Father. (Matthew 16:27)

[He] will come in the same way as you saw Him go into heaven. (Acts 1:11)

Athanasius, Dialog 5, *Of the Trinity* (t. 2, f. 257, ed. Colon.):

According to His good pleasure He made the humanity perfect above its own nature and did not prevent it from being a rational living being ‹, a creature, a true human nature›. (*MPG*, 28:1280–81)

Theophylact, from Chrysostom, on Matthew 28 (p. 184):

I, previously the condemned nature, being God, according to the unconfused union with the Son of God, have received power over all things. (*MPG*, 123:485A; *Theophylact*, 258)

Cyril, book 4, chapter 24 (t. 4, p. 377, and 3, f. 783):

He has shown that His entire body is full of the life-giving energy of the Spirit, not because it has lost the nature of flesh and has been turned into Spirit, but because it is united with Spirit, it has acquired the entire power to make alive. (*MPG*, 73:603B; *Library*, 43:437)

The same author, *Of the Incarnation*, chapter 8:

By way of illustration, think of how fire adheres to a burning coal of wood, so also God the Word, united to humanity, has transformed the received nature into its glory and efficacy. God has been united to humanity in a way that we cannot fully understand, but has conferred on it even the operation of His [divine] nature. (*MPG*, 75:1379; *Library*, 44:194)

Theodoret, Dialogue 2 (t. 4, f. 82 and 112):

The body of the Lord arose, glorified with divine glory and therefore incapable of decay and suffering. It arose immortal and is worshiped by human powers; nevertheless, it is still a body, having the former circumscription. (*MPG*, 83:163A)

The same author, in Dialogue 3, approves this sentence of Apollinarius:

If the nature of iron is not changed when it is mingled with fire to such an extent that the iron is able to do things that pertain to the fire, neither therefore is the union of God with a body a change of the body, although it gives the body the ability to do divine things. (*MPG*, 83:215B)

Damascene, book 3, chapter 17:

The Lord's flesh was enriched with divine operations because of its complete personal union with the Word, but in no way did it experience any loss of those things that belong naturally to it. (*MPG*, 94:1069B; *NPNF*, ser. 2, 9[pt. 2]:66)

The same, book 2, chapter 22:

> Although the Lord's soul by nature did not know the future, nevertheless, because it was personally united to God the Word, it had knowledge of all things, not by grace, but because of the personal union.

And shortly afterward:

> Since the natures in Christ are distinct, the natural wills, that is, the powers of will, are also distinct. (*MPG*, 94:948A/B; *NPNF*, ser. 2, 9[pt. 2]:37)

VIII.

According to its own nature, and because of the personal union, the human nature is a participant in, and capable of, the divine majesty that belongs to God.

For in Him the whole fullness of deity dwells bodily. (Colossians 2:9)

In whom are hidden all the treasures of wisdom and knowledge. (Colossians 2:3)

Justin, in *Expositio Fidei*, p. 182 (f. 389, ed. Colon., 1686]:

> Christ is not in others as He is in the Father, not because He is not in them, but because they are not capable of receiving the Divine as He has.

Also:

> A defiled body does not receive rays of divinity. (*MPG*, 6:1237–39)

And shortly afterwards:

> The Sun of Righteousness is, in substance, present equally to all things, since He is God. We, however, are weak and our eyes are dim because of the filth of sin. We are incapable of receiving the light. His own temple, His own pure eye, is capable of receiving the splendor of all the light, since it has been formed by the Holy Spirit and is altogether separated from sin. (*MPG*, 6:1240)

Origen, *De Principiis*, book 2, chapter 6 (t. 1, op. f. 698 and 749, ed. Basil):

> The entire soul of Christ receives the entire Word. It is received into His light and splendor. (*MPG*, 11:211C; *ANF*, 4:282)

Book 4:

> The soul of Christ, united to the Word of God, is made fully capable of receiving the Son of God. (*MPG*, 11:405D; *ANF*, 4:378)

Augustine, Ep. 57:

> Although God is entirely present to all creatures and dwells especially in believers, they do not entirely receive Him. According to differences in their ability to receive Him, some possess and receive more of Him, and others less. But when it comes to Christ, our Head, the Apostle says, "In Him dwells all the fullness of Deity bodily" (Colossians 2:9). (*MPL*, 33:837, 383, 847; *CSEL*, 52:113, 115–16; *Library*, 30:252)

IX.

It is well known and undeniable that the Godhead, with its divine majesty, is not locally circumscribed [limited] by the flesh as though it were shut up in a container. Athanasius, Origen, Gregory of Nyssa, and others correctly state this, and so does the Book of Concord, which expressly rejects it as an error to teach that the humanity of Christ has been locally expanded into all places, or that, by the personal union, the human nature of Christ has been transformed into an infinite essence. Nevertheless, since the divine and human nature in Christ are personally and inseparably united in Christ, the Holy Scriptures and holy Fathers testify that wherever Christ is, He is not there with only half His person, or with only a part of His person, for instance, the divinity alone, separate and bare, minus and without His assumed humanity, or that He is somehow personally united to it or separated from it, outside of the personal union with the humanity. His entire person, as God and man, according to the mode of the personal union with the humanity, which is an inscrutable mystery, is everywhere present in a way and in a measure that is known to God.

> He who descended is the one who also ascended far above all the heavens, that He might fill all things. (Ephesians 4:10)

Oecumenius explains it this way:

> Long ago He filled all things with His bare divinity. In order to fill all things with His flesh He became incarnate, both descending and ascending. (*MPG*, 118:1217/1220)

Theophylact, on the same passage (*Comment. in Eph.*, p. 535, ed. Lond., 1636):

He fills all things with His dominion and working in the flesh, since even before He had filled all things with His divinity. These things oppose Paul of Samosata and Nestorius. (*MPG*, 124:1083D)

Leo, Epist. 10 (Ep. 24, chapter 5, p. 245, and in Serm., f. 121, ed. cit.):

The Church catholic lives and advances in this faith, that in Christ Jesus we do not believe in the humanity without the true divinity, nor in the divinity without the true humanity. (*MPL, 54:777; NPNF*, ser. 2, 12[pt. 1]:42–43)

The same, in Discourse 3, *On the Passion*:

The catholic faith teaches and requires that we know that in our Redeemer two natures have united and that while their unique properties remain, a union of both substances has taken place since the time that the Word became flesh in the womb of the Blessed Virgin. Therefore, we are not to think of God without thinking that He is man. Nor are we to think of the man, without thinking that He is God.

In the same place:

Each nature, by distinct operations, declares its genuineness. But neither separates itself from connection with the other. Here nothing belonging to the one is lacking to the other. But God assumed the entire man, and so united Himself to man and man to Himself, that each nature is in the other. Neither passed into the other with the loss of its own attributes. (*MPL, 54:319B; NPNF*, ser. 2, 12[pt. 1]:165)

X.

Since the article of Christology is especially intended to direct us to where we should seek and apprehend the entire person of the Mediator, God and man, the Book of Concord, as also all other holy Fathers, directs us not to wood, or stone, or anything else, but to that which Christ has pointed and directed us in His Word.

Cyril, book 2, on John, chapter 32 (t. 3, p. 1063, ed. cit.):

Christ's garments were divided into four parts, but His mantle alone remained undivided. This is a sign of a mystery. The four corners of the earth have been brought to salvation. They share the garment of the Word, that is, His flesh, among themselves in such a way that it is not divided. For the Only-Begotten, passing into each, so to be shared by each, sanctifies their soul and body by His flesh. He is all in all indivisibly and entirely. Because He is one, He is everywhere, but in no way divided. (*MPG*, 74:659B/C)

Theophylact, on John 19 (f. 825, ed. cit.):

The holy body of Christ is indivisible even while it is "divided" and distributed to the four corners of the earth. It is distributed among them individually and sanctifies the soul of each one with the body. The Only-Begotten is by His own flesh in all, entirely and indivisibly because He is everywhere. He has in no way been divided, even as Paul exclaims [Ephesians 4:12]. (*MPG*, 124:278A/B)

Chrysostom (t. 4, p. 1773, ed. Basil. and t. 6, f. 846, ed. Frankf.), Homil. 17, *Ad Ebr.*, p. 16 (and **Ambrose**, chapter 10, *Ad Hebraicos*):

Since He is offered up in many places, are there many Christs? Not at all. The one Christ is everywhere, being completely here and completely there, one body. For as He who is offered in many places is one body, and not many bodies, so is He also one sacrifice. He is that High Priest of ours who has offered the sacrifice that cleanses us. We also now offer that which, having been offered then, was not consumed. This is done in remembrance of that which was done then. "This do," says He, "in remembrance of Me." For we do not make another sacrifice, as the high priest, but always the same. We rather bring about a remembrance of the sacrifice. (Note: This quote is against the propitiatory sacrifice of the papist Mass.) (*MPG*, 63:131; *NPNF*, ser. 1, 14:449)

Conclusion

Christian reader, these testimonies of the ancient teachers of the Church have been provided here not to suggest that our Christian faith is founded on the authority of men. The true saving faith is not founded on any Church teacher, old or new, but only and alone on God's Word, as contained in the Scriptures of the holy prophets and apostles, an unquestionable witness of divine truth. With his special and uncanny crafts, Satan has caused fanatics to lead men from the Holy Scriptures—which, thank God! even a common layman can now read with benefit—to the writings of the Ancient Church, which are like a broad ocean. A person who has not read the Fathers carefully cannot know precisely whether or not these new teachers are quoting their words correctly and thus they leave a person in grievous doubt. This is why we have been compelled to declare, with this

Catalog, and to show everyone that this new false doctrine has as little foundation in the ancient, pure teachers of the Church as in the Holy Scriptures. It is, in fact, diametrically opposed to it. They quote the Church Fathers in such a way as to give them a false meaning, contrary to the Fathers' will. They do this just as they wantonly pervert the simple, plain, and clear words of Christ's testament and the pure testimonies of the Holy Scriptures. Because of this, the Book of Concord directs everyone to the Holy Scriptures and the simple Catechism. The person who clings to this basic form with true, simple faith provides what is best for his soul and conscience, since it is built on a firm and immovable Rock (Matthew 7; 17; Galatians 1; Psalm 119).

Chronology of Christ's Life According to the Gospels

Event	Matthew	Mark	Luke	John
Pre-existence of Christ				1:1–18
Genealogy of Jesus through Joseph	1:1–17			
Genealogy of Jesus through Mary			3:23–38	
Gabriel announces John's birth			1:1–25	
Gabriel visits Mary			1:26–38	
Mary visits Elizabeth, John's mother			1:39–56	
Birth of John the Baptist			1:57–80	
Angel visits Joseph in a dream	1:18–25			
Birth of Jesus in Bethlehem			2:1–7	
Shepherds visit Jesus			2:8–20	
Circumcision of Jesus			2:21	
Jesus presented in the temple			2:22–38	
Wise men bring gifts	2:1–12			
Joseph's family escapes to Egypt	2:13–15			
Herod's wrath on Bethlehem's children	2:16–18			
Joseph's family settles in Nazareth	2:19–23		2:39	
Childhood of Jesus			2:40–52	
Ministry of John the Baptist	3:1–12	1:1–8	3:1–20	
John baptizes Jesus	3:13–17	1:9–11	3:21–22	
Temptation of Jesus	4:1–11	1:12–13	4:1–13	
John's testimony about Christ				1:19–28
John recounts Christ's Baptism				1:29–34
The 1st disciples				1:35–51
The 1st miracle - turning water to wine				2:1–12
The 1st temple cleansing				2:13–25
Nicodemus meets Jesus at night				3:1–21
Disciples baptize many in Judea				3:22–24

Event	Matthew	Mark	Luke	John
Disciples ask John about Jesus				3:25–36
Herod imprisons John the Baptist	4:12	1:14	(3:19–20)	
Jesus withdraws from Judea				4:1–3
Samaritan woman at Jacob's well				4:4–26
Disciples question Jesus				4:27–38
Samaritans come to Jesus				4:39–42
Jesus continues toward Galilee			4:14–15	4:43
The 1st rejection in Nazareth			4:16–30	
Arrival in Cana of Galilee				4:43–45
The 2nd miracle - Official's son healed				4:46–54
Jesus settles in Capernaum	4:13–17	1:14–15	4:31–32	
Fishermen called to be disciples	4:18–22	1:16–20		
Demoniac in Capernaum synagogue		1:21–28	4:33–37	
Peter's mother-in-law healed	8:14–17	1:29–31	4:38–39	
Many healed at sunset		1:32–34	4:40–41	
Disciples seek Jesus		1:35–38	4:42–43	
Jesus preaches in the synagogues	4:23–25	1:39	4:44	
Jesus preaches in Simon's boat			5:1–3	
Miraculous catch of fish			5:4–11	
Jesus heals a leper	8:2–4	1:40–45	5:12–16	
Jesus cures a paralytic	9:2–8	2:1–12	5:17–26	
Matthew (Levi) called to be a disciple	9:9	2:13–14	5:27–28	
Parables at Levi's reception	9:10–17	2:15–22	5:29–39	
Jesus in Jerusalem at the 2nd Passover				5:1
Man healed at pools of Bethesda				5:2–15
Jesus challenged for healing on Sabbath				5:16–47
Disciples pick grain on the Sabbath	12:1–8	2:23–28	6:1–5	
Man's hand healed on the Sabbath	12:9–14	3:1–6	6:6–11	
Jesus withdraws to the sea	12:14–21	3:7		
Many follow Jesus to be healed	4:23–25	3:7–12		
Jesus prays on a mountain			6:12	
Jesus selects 12 disciples		3:13–19	6:13–16	

Event	Matthew	Mark	Luke	John
Jesus descends and heals the multitude			6:17–19	
Jesus ascends to address the multitude	5:1			
Sermon on the Mount	5:1–8:1		6:20–49	
Jesus heals a centurion's servant	8:5–13		7:1–10	
Widow of Nain's son is raised			7:11–17	
John sends 2 disciples to question Jesus	11:2–6		7:18–23	
Jesus commends John the Baptist	11:7–19		7:24–35	
Jesus rebukes 3 cities	11:20–30			
Jesus dines with Simon the Pharisee			7:36–50	
Generous women			8:1–3	
Jesus heals a demon-possessed man	12:22–23	3:20–22		
Pharisees rebuked	12:24–37	3:22–30		
The sign of Jonah	12:38–45			
Family seeks Jesus	12:46–50	3:31–35	8:19–21	
Parables by the sea	13:1–35	4:1–34	8:4–18	
Parables explained and told in private	13:36–53			
Orders to cross the Sea of Galilee	8:18	4:35	8:22	
Jesus calms a stormy sea	8:23–27	4:36–41	8:23–25	
Legion cast out of violent man	8:28–34	5:1–20	8:26–39	
Jesus sails to Capernaum	9:1	5:21	8:40	
Jairus asks Jesus to heal his daughter	9:18–19	5:22–23	8:41–42	
Ill woman is healed by touching Jesus	9:20–22	5:24–34	8:42–48	
Daughter's death is reported to Jairus		5:35–36	8:49–50	
Jesus raises Jairus's daughter to life	9:23–26	5:37–43	8:51–56	
Jesus heals two blind men	9:27–31			
Jesus heals a mute demoniac	9:32–34			
The 2nd rejection in Nazareth	13:54–58	6:1–6		
12 sent out to preach	9:35–11:1	6:7–13	9:1–6	
Death of John the Baptist	14:1–12			
Herod fears John the Baptist has risen		6:14–29	9:7–9	
12 return and they withdraw	14:13	6:30–32	9:10	6:1
Jesus teaches and heals the multitude	14:14	6:33–34	9:11	6:2

Event	Matthew	Mark	Luke	John
Jesus feeds 5,000	14:15–21	6:35–44	9:12–17	6:3–14
Jesus prays alone	14:22–23	6:45–47		6:15
Jesus walks on water	14:24–27	6:48–52		6:16–21
Peter walks on water, then sinks	14:28–33			
Healings in Gennesaret	14:34–36	6:53–56		
Bread of life discourse				6:22–7:1
Traditions of men rebuked	15:1–11	7:1–16		
Parable explained in private	15:12–20	7:17–23		
Gentile woman's faith	15:21–28	7:24–30		
Jesus heals a deaf man		7:31–37		
Many healed on a mountain	15:29–31			
Jesus feeds 4,000	15:32–39	8:1–10		
Pharisees seek a sign	16:1–4	8:11–13		
Leaven of the Pharisees	16:5–12	8:13–21		
Blind man cured in Bethsaida		8:22–26		
Peter confesses that Jesus is the Christ	16:13–20	8:27–30		
Jesus rebukes Peter	16:21–28	8:31–9:1	9:18–27	
The transfiguration	17:1–8	9:2–8	9:28–36	
Elijah discussed while descending	17:9–13	9:9–13		
Demon is cast out of boy	17:14–18	9:14–27	9:37–43	
Disciples ask about the miracle	17:19–21	9:28–29		
Jesus discusses His death	17:22–23	9:30–32	9:44–45	
Jesus pays temple tax with a miracle	17:24–27			
Disciples argue about who is the great-est	18:1–6	9:33–37	9:46–48	
John's zeal without understanding		9:38–42	9:49–50	
Warnings about stumbling blocks	18:7–11	9:43–50		
Parable about the lost sheep	18:12–14			
Instructions on church discipline	18:15–20			
Peter's question about forgiveness	18:21–35			
Feast of Booths at hand				7:2
Brothers advise Jesus to go to Judea				7:3–8
Jesus stays in Galilee				7:9

Event	Matthew	Mark	Luke	John
Jesus sets His face to go to Jerusalem			9:51	7:10
Messengers sent to Samaria to prepare way			9:52–53	
James and John rebuked for attitude			9:54–56	
Unfit followers	8:19–22		9:57–62	
People afraid to speak publicly of Jesus				7:11–13
Jesus in the temple mid-feast				7:14–15
Jesus says some seek to kill Him				7:16–19
Defense for healing on Sabbath				7:20–24
Jesus cries out in the temple				7:25–30
Multitudes amazed at signs				7:31
Pharisees seek to seize Jesus				7:32–36
Last day of feast				7:37
Rivers of living water				7:37–39
Division among the people				7:40–44
Pharisees question officers				7:45–47
Judgement of Nicodemus				7:48–53
Jesus goes to the Mount of Olives				8:1
Teaches at temple in the morning				8:2
Adulterous woman brought to Jesus				8:3–11
Light of the world				8:12–20
Sent by the Father				8:21–30
Temple debate about father Abraham				8:31–59
Jesus leaves the temple				8:59
Jesus heals a man born blind				9:1–7
Neighbors question the former blind man				9:8–12
Pharisees question man's parents				9:13–34
Jesus finds the man				9:35–39
Pharisees ask if they are blind				9:40–10:6
Jesus explains He is the Good Shepherd				10:7–18
Division among the Jews				10:19–21
Seventy sent out			10:1–16	

Event	Matthew	Mark	Luke	John
Seventy return			10:17–20	
Jesus rejoices			10:21–22	
Jesus privately blesses the 12			10:23–24	
Lawyer tests Jesus			10:25–28	
Parable of the Good Samaritan			10:29–37	
Martha prepares while Mary listens			10:38–42	
Jesus teaches the disciples how to pray			11:1–13	
Blasphemy and teachings on demons			11:14–26	
A woman blesses Mary			11:27–28	
Sign of Jonah			11:29–32	
The lamp of the body			11:33–36	
Lunch with a Pharisee			11 37	
Jesus does not wash His hands			11:38	
Jesus pronounces woes on the Pharisees			11:39–44	
Jesus pronounces woes on the lawyers			11:45–52	
Jesus leaves, and they plot against Him			11:53–54	
Jesus teaches a great crowd			12:1–12	
Jesus warns against greed			12:13–15	
Parables about being ready			12:16–40	
Peter's question			12:41	
More parables			12:42–59	
Fate of Galileans reported to Jesus			13:1–5	
Parable of the fig tree			13:6–9	
Woman healed on the Sabbath			13:10–13	
Synagogue official opposes Jesus			13:14–17	
Parables of mustard seed and leaven			13:18–21	
Feast of Dedication in the temple				10:22–23
Jews confront Christ				10:24–39
Jesus goes to Aenon near Salim				10:40–42
Jesus travels toward Jerusalem			13:22	
How many will be saved?			13:23–30	
Pharisees warn Jesus about Herod			13:31–35	

Event	Matthew	Mark	Luke	John
In a Pharisee's house on the Sabbath			14:1	
Man with dropsy healed			14:2–6	
Parable of the guests			14:7–11	
Parable to the host of the feast			14:12–14	
Parable of the dinner			14:15–24	
Great multitudes travel with Jesus			14:25	
The cost of discipleship			14:25–35	
Eats with tax collectors and sinners			15:1–2	
Lost sheep, coin, and son			15:3–32	
Parable of the unrighteous steward			16:1–13	
Pharisees scoff; teaching on divorce			16:14–18	
The rich man and Lazarus			16:19–31	
Jesus instructs disciples			17:1–10	
Lazarus of Bethany reported sick				11:1–6
Jesus delays for 2 days				11:6
Jesus prepares 12 to go to Judea				11:7–16
Arrives near Bethany, 2 days later				11:17–18
Martha meets Jesus				11:19–29
Mary comes to Jesus				11:30–37
Jesus comes to the tomb				11:38
Jesus raises Lazarus from the dead				11:39–44
Unbelievers report to Pharisees				11:45–46
Conspiracy to kill Jesus				11:47–53
Jesus goes to Ephraim				11:54
Ten lepers are cleansed			17:11–14	
Samaritan returns to thank Jesus			17:15–19	
Pharisees ask about the Kingdom			17:20–21	
Jesus warns disciples about the future			17:22–37	
Parable of the unjust judge			18:1–8	
Parable of the Pharisee and tax collector			18:9–14	
Jesus goes to Judea by the Jordan	19:1	10:1		
Multitudes follow Jesus	19:2			

Event	Matthew	Mark	Luke	John
Pharisees question Jesus about divorce	19:3–9	10:2–9		
Disciples question Jesus about divorce	19:10–12	10:10–12		
Jesus blesses little children	19:13–15	10:13–16	18:15–17	
Rich young ruler	19:16–26	10:17–27	18:18–27	
Disciples reward	19:27–30	10:28–31	18:28–30	
First shall be last discourse	20:1–16			
Jesus predicts death on road to Jerusalem	20:17–19	10:32–34	18:31–34	
Request for James and John	20:20–24	10:35–41		
Relationship of disciples to each other	20:25–28	10:42–45		
Blind men healed near Jericho	20:29–34	10:46–52	18:35–43	
Zacchaeus is converted near Jericho			19:1–10	
Jesus is near Jerusalem			19:11	
Blind men healed near Jericho			19:12–27	
Journey toward Jerusalem for Passover				11:54
Jesus discussed by Jews and priests				11:55–57
Jesus in Bethany				12:1
Mary anoints Jesus in Simon's house				12:2–8
Mary's deed recounted	26:6–13	14:3–9		
Crowds come to see Jesus and Lazarus				12:9
Chief priests conspire to kill Lazarus				12:10–11
Jesus ascends toward Jerusalem	21:1	11:1	19:28	
Two disciples get a colt	21:1–7	11:1–7	19:29–35	
Triumphal entry into Jerusalem	21:8–11	11:7–10	19:35–38	12:12–18
Pharisees' reaction			19:39–40	12:19
Jesus weeps for Jerusalem			19:41–44	
Jesus enters Jerusalem then goes to Bethany		11:11		
Jesus curses a fig tree		11:12–14		
The 2nd temple cleansing	21:12–13	11:15–17	19:45–46	
Jesus heals many in the temple	21:14			
Jewish leaders seek to destroy Jesus	21:15–16	11:18	19:47–48	
Jesus leaves Jerusalem	21:17	11:19		

Event	Matthew	Mark	Luke	John
The withered fig tree (next morning)	21:18–22	11:20–26		
Authority challenged in the temple	21:23–27	11:27–33	20:1–8	
Parable of the two sons	21:28–32			
Parable of the vine growers	21:33–46	12:1–12	20:9–18	
Parable of the wedding feast	22:1–14			
Jews question on paying taxes	22:15–22	12:13–17	20:19–26	
Sadducees question the resurrection	22:23–33	12:18–27	20:27–40	
Scribes and Pharisees question Jesus	22:34–40	12:28–34		
Jesus questions them about who He is	22:41–46	12:35–37	20:41–44	
Warnings about Scribes and Pharisees	23:1–39	12:38–40	20:45–47	
The widow's mite		12:41–44	21:1–4	
Disciples admire the temple	24:1–2	13:1–2	21:5–6	
4 fishermen question Jesus	24:3	13:3–4	21:7	
Jesus warns disciples of persecution	24:4–14	13:5–13	21:8–19	
Jesus predicts the fall of Jerusalem	24:15–28	13:14–23	21:20–24	
Jesus teaches about the 2nd coming	24:29–31	13:24–27	21:25–28	
Parable of the fig tree	24:32–33	13:28–29	21:29–31	
Warnings to be alert	24:34–51	13:30–37	21:32–36	
Parable of the 10 virgins	25:1–13			
Parable of the talents	25:14–30			
Warnings about the judgment	25:31–46			
Jesus predicts day of crucifixion	26:1–2			
People come early to hear Jesus teach			21:37–38	
Greeks seek Jesus				12:20–22
Final public appeals to unbelievers				12:23–50
Plot to kill Jesus	26:3–5	14:1–2	22:1–2	
Judas bargains to betray Jesus	26:14–16	14:10–11	22:3–6	
Peter & John sent to prepare for Passover	26:17–19	14:12–16	22:7–13	
Fellowship in the upper room	26:20	14:17	22:14	
Jesus washes the disciples' feet				13:1–20

Event	Matthew	Mark	Luke	John
The Lord's Supper	26:26–29	14:22–25	22:14–20	1 Cor. 11:23–29
Jesus predicts His betrayal	26:21–25	14:18–21	22:21–23	13:21–26
Judas leaves				13:27–30
A new commandment				13:31–35
Dispute about the greatest disciple			22:24–30	
Jesus predicts the disciples' denial	26:31–32	14:27–28		
Jesus tells Simon He prayed for him			22:31–32	
Jesus predicts Peter's denials	26:33–35	14:29–31	22:33–34	13:36–38
Jesus warns the disciples to be prepared			22:35–38	
Jesus comforts the disciples				14:1–4
Jesus responds to Thomas				14:5–7
Jesus responds to Philip				14:8–21
Jesus responds to Judas not Iscariot				14:22–31
They sing a hymn and leave	26:30	14:26		14:31
The farewell discourse				15:1–16:33
Jesus prays for His disciples				17:1–26
The fellowship enters Gethsemane	26:36	14:32		18:1
Jesus prays in the Garden of Gethsemane	26:36–46	14:32–42	22:40–46	
Mob comes to arrest Jesus	26:47	14:43		18:2–3
Judas betrays Jesus with a kiss	26:48–50	14:44–45	22:47–48	
Jesus answers the mob with authority				18:4–9
Peter severs the ear of Malchus	26:50–54	14:46–47	22:49–50	18:10–11
Jesus heals the high priest's servant			22:51	
Jesus is arrested; the disciples flee	26:55–56	14:48–52	22:52–54	18:12
Jesus led to high priest's house	26:57	14:53	22:54	18:13–14
Peter follows at a distance	26:58	14:54	22:54	18:15–16
Peter's 1st denial - doorkeeping girl	26:69–70	14:66–68	22:55–57	18:17–18
Annas questions Jesus				18:19–24
Peter's 2nd denial - by the fire	26:71–72	14:69–70	22:58	18:25
Peter's 3rd denial - relative of Malchus	26:73–75	14:70–72	22:59–62	18:26–27

Event	Matthew	Mark	Luke	John
Guards beat Jesus			22:63–65	
False witnesses testify	26:59–61	14:55–59		
Caiaphas condemns Jesus	26:62–66	14:60–64	22:66–71	
Sanhedrin beats Jesus	26:67–68	14:65		
Jesus led from Caiaphas to Praetorium				18:28
Remorse of Judas	27:1–10		Acts 1:16–20	
Jesus before Pilate	27:1–2, 11–14		23:1–7	18:29–38
Jesus before Herod			23:8–10	
Herod's soldiers mock Jesus		15:1–5	23:11–12	
Pilate releases Barabbas	27:15–26	15:6–15	23:13–25	18:38–40
Pilate's soldiers crown and mock Jesus	27:27–31	15:16–20		19:1–3
Pilate tries to release Jesus				19:4–7
Pilate questions Jesus again				19:8–11
Pilate tries to release Jesus again				19:12
Pilate sentences Jesus				19:13–15
Pilate delivers Jesus to be crucified				19:16
Jesus carries the cross				19:17
Simon of Cyrene bears the cross	27:32	15:20–21	23:26	
Jesus speaks to weeping women			23:27–32	
Jesus is brought to Golgotha	27:33	15:22	23:32–33	19:17
Soldiers offer Jesus sour wine mix	27:34	15:23		
He is crucified on the 3rd hour		15:25		
2 robbers are crucified with Jesus	27:38	15:27–28	23:33	19:18
Inscription written by Pilate	27:37	15:26	23:38	19:19–22
"Forgive them…"			23:34	
Soldiers divide the garments of Jesus	27:35–36	15:24	23:34	19:23–24
"Behold, your mother!"				19:25–27
Multitudes mock Jesus	27:39–43	15:29–32	23:35–37	
Robbers mock Jesus	27:44	15:32	23:39	
One robber rebukes the other			23:40–41	
". . . you will be with Me in Paradise."			23:43	

Event	Matthew	Mark	Luke	John
Darkness from 6th to 9th hour	27:45	15:33	23:44–45	
"Eloi, Eloi, lema, sabachthani?"	27:46	15:34		
"I thirst."				19:28
Jesus is offered sour wine on a reed	27:47–49	15:35–36		19:29–30
"It is finished."				19:30
Jesus cries out	27:50	15:37	23:46	
"Into Thy hands I commit My spirit."			23:46	
Jesus bows His head and dies	27:50	15:37	23:46	19:30
Temple veil torn from top to bottom	27:51	15:38	23:45	
Earthquake	27:51			
Saints rise after Christ's resurrection	27:52–53			
Centurion glorifies God	27:54	15:39	23:47	
Multitude leaves grieving			23:48	
Women watch from a distance	27:55–56	15:40–41	23:49	
Request that legs be broken				19:31–32
Soldier pierces Jesus' side				19:33–34
Fulfilment of prophecy				19:35–37
Joseph requests body from Pilate	27:57–58	15:42–43	23:50–52	19:38
Centurion reports that Jesus is dead		15:44–45		
Joseph takes the body		15:45		19:38
Nicodemus and Joseph prepare the body				19:39–40
Body placed in new garden tomb	27:59–60	15:46	23:53	19:41–42
Two Marys watch the burial	27:61	15:47	23:54–55	
Roman soldiers guard the tomb	27:62–66			
Two Marys prepare spices and then rest			23:56	
Angel rolls stone	28:2–4			
Women bring spices to tomb at dawn	28:1	16:1–4	24:1–3	20:1
Angels appear to women	28:5–7	16:5–7	24:4–8	
Women run to tell disciples	28:8	16:8	24:9–11	20:2
Peter and John inspect the empty tomb			24:12	20:3–9
Peter and John go home			24:12	20:10
Mary Magdalene stands weeping				20:11

Event	Matthew	Mark	Luke	John
Mary sees two angels				20:12–13
Jesus appears to Mary Magdalene		16:9		20:14–17
Jesus appears to other women	28:9–10			
Women report to the disciples		16:10–11		20:18
Guards report to the priests	28:11–15			
Jesus meets 2 on road to Emmaus		16:12–13	24:13–32	
Jesus appears to Simon Peter	1 Cor 15:5		24:34	
Two report to disciples in Jerusalem			24:33–35	
Jesus appears to disciples without Thomas			24:36–46	20:19–24
Disciples report to Thomas				20:25
Jesus appears to disciples and Thomas		16:14		20:26–29
Jesus appears to seven by the sea				21:1–14
Jesus questions Peter 3 times				21:15–23
Jesus appears to 500 brethren	1 Cor 15:6			
Jesus appears to James	1 Cor 15:7			
Jesus commissions the apostles	28:16–20	16:15–18	24:44–49	
Jesus is received into heaven		16:19–20	24:50–53	
John's first testimony				20:30–31
John's second testimony				21:24–25
Luke summarizes the 40-day appearances			Acts 1:4–11	

For Further Study

For further detailed study of Christology, the following resources are recommended:

Aloys Grillmeier, *Christ in Christian Tradition: Volume I: From the Apostolic Age to Chalcedon*, Translated by John Bowden (Atlanta: John Knox Press, 1988).

Athanasius, *On the Incarnation of the Word of God* (with an introduction by C. S. Lewis), Translated by John Behr (Yonkers: St. Vladimir's Seminary Press, 2012).

Anselm, *Why God Became Man?* In *Anselm of Canterbury: The Major Works* (New York: Oxford University Press, 2008).

Christology of the Later Fathers: Library of Christian Classics, Edited by Edward Harty (Nashville: Westminster Press, 1995).

Concordia: The Lutheran Confessions: A Reader's Edition of the Book of Concord, Second Edition, General Editor Paul T. McCain (St. Louis: Concordia, 2006).

Glossary

apostle. From the Greek word *apostolos*, meaning "to send." The one sent goes with the full authority of the sender. The apostles were called and sent directly by Jesus.

atonement. From an old French term for being "at one." Reconciliation between parties that were previously divided. One man's life given as a sacrifice and ransom to redeem all others.

blasphemy. From the Greek word *blasphemia,* which means "to slander." To commit blasphemy is to lie about the most important thing in the world: God and His Word.

Christ: Greek for "Messiah." The title for Jesus that identifies Him as the one set apart by God to fulfill the Old Testament prophecies of a Savior.

Communicatio Idiomatum. Latin for "communication of properties." This is the teaching that the attributes of both the divine and human natures are ascribed to the one person of Jesus.

confession. The act by which one admits or confesses sin(s) and the guilt of sin.

exaltation: The resumption and continuation of such full and constant use of His divine attributes according to His human nature was and is the exaltation of Christ (Ephesians 4:8; Hebrews 2:7).

Gospel. The message of Christ's death and resurrection for the forgiveness of sins, eternal life, and salvation. The Holy Spirit works through the Gospel in Word and Sacrament to create and sustain faith and to empower good works. The Gospel is found in both the Old and New Testaments.

grace. The unearned and undeserved gift of forgiveness and eternal life received by faith and given to all who believe. Ephesians 2:8–9 shows us that this gift is free to those who receive it but was purchased at great cost by Jesus' life, death on the cross, and resurrection.

humiliation: Christ humbled Himself by not exercising fully, according to His human nature, the rights and powers that rightfully belonged to Him as the Son of God. Christ humbled Himself according to His human nature. The divine nature was not capable of being humbled or exalted or changed in any other way in state or condition.

hypostatic union. Theological term for the union of the two natures (divine and human) in the person of Jesus. They are separate yet act as a unit in the one person of Jesus. Jesus is God in flesh (John 1:1, 14; 10:30–33; 20:28; Philippians 2:5–8; Hebrews 1:8). He is fully God and fully man (Colossians 2:9). Therefore, there is a "union in one person of a full human nature and a full divine nature."

incarnation. Literally, being embodied in flesh or taking on flesh. Jesus Christ's incarnation occurred within Mary's womb and continues to this day. This is why we can call Him the God-man: because as God He took on human flesh fully and completely.

Jesus. It means "Yahweh saves." The name given the incarnate Son of God (Matthew 1:20–21; Luke 1:31–38); the second Person of the Trinity; the object of Christian faith, the way, the truth, and the life apart from whom nobody comes to the Father (Acts 4:12).

Judgment Day. The day of Christ's return at which time will be the end of the world and the bodily resurrection of all mankind. Christ the Judge, who knows all things, will proceed at once to pronounce sentence by judicial and final separation. Believers (righteous) will be awarded the everlasting kingdom prepared for them by Himself, as an inheritance (Galatians 3:26–29). The unbelievers (unrighteous) will be condemned to everlasting punishment (Matthew 25:24–46).

Last Day. See *Judgment Day*.

Lord: From the Greek *Kyrios*, used with the name of Jesus to indicate that He is both Lord and God. Indicates He is true man and true God.

Means of Grace. The means by which God gives us the forgiveness, life, and salvation won by the death and resurrection of Christ: God's Word, Absolution, Baptism, and the Lord's Supper.

miracle: From the Latin *mirus* which means "wonderful." A miracle is the cessation of the normal way of nature. Jesus' miracles signaled that He was something unique. In the New Testament, the "miracles" are often called "signs."

sin. Betraying God; rejecting His will and His ways; any thought, word, or deed that departs from the will of God.

sinful nature. Our human nature, after the fall, is thoroughly corrupted by sin, making us God's enemies and lovers of ourselves.

testament. A will that establishes the disposition of one's belongings at the time of death, or a covenant established by God between God and man. The Lord's Supper fulfills both definitions: prior to the cross, Jesus leaves Christians His body and blood for the forgiveness of their sins; and this sacrament is a part of His covenant of grace for man.

tetragrammaton: Greek for "the four letters," a term used to describe the personal name of God in Hebrew, יהוה, and commonly transliterated into Latin letters as YHWH.

Trinity, triune. One true God in three persons: Father, Son, and Holy Spirit.

vicarious satisfaction. The teaching that Jesus Christ is our substitute before God, who takes the punishment that our sins deserve and satisfies the perfect will and commands of God for us, in our place, on our behalf.

Scripture Index

NEW TESTAMENT

For additional Gospel references, see the charts on pp. 70, 181–93.